ONE STEP BEHIND
MANDELA

ONE STEP BEHIND
MANDELA

THE STORY OF **RORY STEYN**,
NELSON MANDELA'S CHIEF BODYGUARD,
AS TOLD TO **DEBORA PATTA**

ZEBRA

Published by Zebra Press
(an imprint of the New Holland Struik Publishing Group (Pty) Ltd)
PO Box 5563, Rivonia, 2128
Tel: 27 11 807 2292
Fax: 27 11 803 1783
E-mail: marikat@struik.co.za

First edition, first impression June 2000

Copy editors Tracey Chalmers & Jacqui Greenop
Cover designer Lindy Truswell
Book designer Denise Meredith
DTP Denise Meredith

Printed and bound by Trident

ISBN 1-86872-269-4

This book is dedicated to my two sons, Kyle and Iain.
Seek the truth my boys,
'and the truth will set you free.' (John 8:32)
Rory Steyn

*   *   *   *   *   *

In loving memory of Giuseppe Patta.
Debora Patta

ACKNOWLEDGEMENTS

As is the case with the writing of any book, there are always so many people who contributed in so many ways and they have all ultimately been a part of what is now this book.

First of all, I need to say a big thank-you to my co-author, Debora Patta. I asked Debora to write my story for me for three reasons. Firstly because she's a woman and I wanted a female perspective on this work. Secondly because as a political journalist, she was particularly close to the political process spanning the period prior to and including President Mandela's term of office. And thirdly because Mandela both knows and likes her. I have to say that I made the right choice. Working with you has been a pleasure, Debs; and I admire the fact that the majority of our book was written while you were preparing to and had become a mother for the first time. I wish you, Mweli and Chiara happiness and joy.

To Madiba, for all he taught me, for the support and goodwill we as his protectors received from him and his family. *Siyabonga, Tata.*

Then to my many colleagues who contributed to a large or small degree, with stories, anecdotes and just their enthusiasm for the book: Gary Kruser, Jason Tshabalala, Sam Shitlabane, Des van Rooyen, Selby Masikane, Johan Scott, Hermann Coetzee, Quintin Henwick and Popi Lukhele – all from the Presidential Protection Unit (PPU).

Also Stan Downey of the Special Branch, London Metropolitan Police Service, for chasing down that elusive photograph.

My dear friend Zelda la Grange from the Office of the President as well as Sasje Fourie and Andreas Swart from the Department of Foreign Affairs, State Visits and Ceremonial Affairs.

To the photographers whose work is an irreplaceable complement to this book and a compliment to themselves and their skill: Rajesh Jantilal, Adil Bradlow, Schalk van Zuydam, Benny

Gool, Peter Lynch and Dr Dirk de Lange, the doctor/tourist, for the previously unpublished photos taken in Libya.

To Dad for editing the text and supporting the idea. To Mom for coming up with the title.

To all my friends and family who gave their support and prayers for this work.

Lastly, to my long-suffering wife, Gill, for her patience and for keeping the boys out of my hair at times. I love you very much.

And finally to the Tri-Une God whom I serve. Everything happens for a reason and I thank Him for the privilege of allowing me to serve President Mandela during this unique and historic chapter in our beloved country's history.

Rory Steyn
Johannesburg
September 1999

When Rory first mentioned this book to me, it was mid-1998. At the time I thought the idea was brilliant but knew that of the many people keen to write a book, very few did. It was another nine months before we spoke about it again. By now I was six months pregnant and had a major election looming, which, as a television correspondent, I would be integrally involved in covering. Nevertheless, I jumped at the chance to co-write this book, knowing that it was a wonderful story that needed to be told. And although I was writing the last chapters with a new-born baby clinging to me, I have not regretted that decision. Thanks, Rory, it was an honour and a privilege to collaborate on this project with you. Your unfailing enthusiasm and respect for me always spurred me on. I have thoroughly enjoyed this experience and wish you all the luck in your new career. You deserve everything of the best.

Thanks to Radio 702's Yusuf Abramjee.

To Nelson Mandela and Graça Machel. You are my modern-day hero and heroine. And every minute I have spent in your company has been both a deep honour and a great joy.

To my mother, Jennifer Patta, thanks for believing in me. It's the greatest gift you could have given me. To Rex and Seth Mzizi, you are the perfect parents-in-law and your support has been invaluable. To my sister Gabriella Patta and good friends Debbie Meyer and Cynthia Allie, I don't know what I would have done without those long, encouraging (and sometimes expensive) telephone chats.

And to Monica Ngebane – I am deeply grateful for those long hours of baby-sitting and the calm and wonderful way you take care of my baby daughter.

Finally to my husband, Mweli Mzizi, and beautiful new daughter, Chiara Nkanyezi. I love you both with all my heart. Your unfailing support and care has helped me all the way and I look forward to finally enjoying many happy family days ahead.

Debora Patta
Johannesburg
September 1999

A special word of thanks to David Kan, CEO of Mustek Electronics, for his unstinting support of this book. The entire process of writing this book was conducted between the two of us using Mecer notebook computers. We are forever in your debt for providing us with the kind of technology that enabled us to complete this book literally from any corner of the globe. Also, the stunning colour photograph section appears courtesy of Mecer computer hardware.

And lastly, to the wonderful team at Zebra Press: Marika Truter, for believing in our project, Tracey Chalmers and Nelisiwe Zondi for making this book happen, Lorna Hiles, for endless patience and photo searches, Lee Cahill, Suzanne Weil, Zenani, Bev, Bryen, Connie Nel and Pamela Wood, for a fantastic marketing and publicity campaign.

Rory & Debora

PREFACE

One step Behind Mandela was conceived long before Nelson Mandela retired as President of South Africa.

But this book was never intended to be a chronological or biographical account of Mandela's life. Hence you will find that this book has been drawn together under a number of themes as opposed to a blow-by-blow account of the Mandela presidency. It is a collection of stories about a great leader and an even greater person. Stories of how he touched people's lives both those closest to him and those who have never even met him. These stories are woven into the different themes and you will often find a tale about Mandela after he stepped down as head of state alongside one that dates prior to his presidency. The time period is not the issue but rather the point the stories are making about the man behind the headlines.

Furthermore this book was never intended to be a tell-all, secret account of Mandela's life. There are many things that the authors have deliberately left out of this book, not because of self-censorship but out of respect for Mandela's private life. Nelson Mandela always has and always will be an immensely private person and it was not our intention to chip away at that protective layer. Instead we hope that we have contributed to the picture of Mandela by providing deeper insights into a fascinating life.

I met Rory Steyn in 1996, shortly after he began serving as Mandela's team leader. At the time he was a Lieutenant-Colonel but due to the new dispensation in South Africa the police force was quickly demilitarised and Rory became a superintendent. Equal rank and status but a more modern way to describe them. Our paths were to cross more frequently in the years that followed. As a political journalist I was frequently assigned to cover the Mandela presidency and in addition I had my own developing relationship with both Mandela and his soon to be wife

Graca Machel. I was fortunate in being allowed to visit both these great leaders in their home setting on many an occasion. And this is reflected in the book where Rory's story finally mixes with mine in the final chapter of this book – *Mandela in Love*. In addition to Rory's observations, I have added my own and so the book becomes more personal. We felt that some of these stories were just too charming to leave out of the book and so in that chapter you need to read both Rory and Debora's account of a grand love affair.

Debora Patta
March 2000

CONTENTS

PROLOGUE

The door to the President's office in Pretoria's Union Buildings opened. Nelson Mandela stepped out, his face set – grim and pensive. He had just concluded the meeting that was to decide Rory Steyn's future as the leader of one of his presidential security teams.

This September 1996 meeting had come about after the circulation of a National Intelligence Report. The document was damning. It cited an allegation made by an apartheid-era Security Branch officer, Paul Erasmus, that Steyn had been involved in the 1988 bombing of Khotso House (the headquarters of the anti-apartheid aligned South African Council of Churches [SACC]). It was true that Steyn had been a member of the Security Branch. True too that he'd been actively involved in the harassment of senior anti-apartheid activists. In fact Steyn was a typical white, conservative South African policeman, who was flattered that he'd been identified at such a young age to do his bit for *volk en vaderland*.

But although he would have jumped at the chance in the past to serve his country in more sinister ways, he did not have blood on his hands. And even though he'd been trained in explosives and bomb disposal, he was never part of the crack apartheid squad that blew up the South African Council of Churches headquarters. This had all been explained to the Director of the National Protection Service, Gary Kruser; but the Presidential Protection Unit (PPU) was an elite unit, made up of South Africa's brightest and best. Black and white officers served side by side. And to them was entrusted the demanding work of protecting Nelson Mandela – one of the most famous people in the world. Adored by millions, hated by some. A man who, because of his courageous fight against apartheid, still had many enemies.

Enemies who could at any stage make a desperate attempt on his life. Nothing could be left to chance. And every single man and woman who served on that Presidential Protection Unit had to be completely above suspicion. The slightest whisper of a scandal meant only one thing – instant dismissal. And Steyn was, after all, a white police officer with an ugly past. The matter had to be taken up at the highest level. A top-level delegation of Steyn's bosses met with the President. Their recommendation – Steyn should be booted out of the Presidential Protection Unit.

Waiting anxiously outside the President's office was Steyn himself. He'd been granted one final request. Should the President want him removed, he would at least have the opportunity to put his case to the leader. This would be his last chance to speak to the President before departing in disgrace.

Upon seeing Steyn sitting in his secretary's office, the President's demeanour changed instantly. A smile lit up his face; and as if nothing had happened, he exclaimed, 'Yes, Rory! Did you enjoy your trip to London?' (The President was referring to his state visit to the UK in 1996. Steyn had been the officer in charge of co-ordinating security.)

The matter was not spoken of again for twelve months. What Rory Steyn did not know then was that at that time the President was not aware that his senior bodyguard had not been involved in the bombing. Mandela firmly believed that Steyn had committed a crime. But in the spirit of the new South Africa he was convinced he deserved a second chance. And so it was that Steyn remained on as Team Leader in Nelson Mandela's security team throughout one of the most exciting periods of South African history.

With deep emotion, Steyn recalls, *I knew that the President had reacted in the manner that I hoped so much for. My position in the unit was not in danger. I realised with absolute conviction that I would, if necessary, lay down my life for this man I had once regarded as a terrorist.*

1

The Path to Forgiveness

Look, I am going in there. Your job is to
protect me, not to tell me what to do.
(Mandela to his bodyguards on being advised
against entering a danger zone.)

Cocktail glasses clinked. Trays of hot and cold snacks were circulating. The talk was of the astonishing events of the past few weeks. The venue – the American ambassador's plush Waterkloof residence in Pretoria. It was March of 1990 and South Africa stood on the brink of a remarkable era. The guest of honour – the man at the centre of it all – was Nelson Mandela, the African National Congress leader, who was later to be president, and who just five weeks earlier had walked out of prison a free man after 27 years behind bars.

The country was still to get used to him. For now, there were many whites who regarded him as a terrorist. And many who fervently believed that the State President, FW de Klerk, was a traitor for having released him from jail unconditionally. After all, Mandela had been convicted of sabotage and had never formally renounced violence.

It was thoughts like these that were going through the mind of Rory Steyn. A former Security Branch officer, he was now the commander of the Johannesburg VIP Protection Unit of the South African Police. It was a tightly closed squad, with the responsibility of ensuring the safety of all VIPs visiting Johannesburg, including State President De Klerk.

Steyn was an invited guest at this reception following the successful protection operation of Marilyn Quayle, wife of US Vice-President Dan Quayle, but he was still armed and ready for action. Mandela was seated in a lounge, deep in conversation with his hosts. *Security is so lax, it would be so easy to murder him,* Steyn mused idly.

Although he had no intention of doing anything of the kind, Steyn was bitter. 'Whites have nothing to fear from the ANC,' was the message the newly unbanned, exiled organisation was seeking to portray. And its Freedom Charter boldly proclaimed, 'South Africa is for all her people, black and white.' *Nothing but ANC propaganda,* Steyn thought with contempt.

But four years after Mandela's release, that 'propaganda' was all true. South Africa had indeed become a country for all her people, as black and white went to the polls in April 1994 in a quiet, dignified manner that astounded the world. And just days later, Steyn once again found himself observing Mandela – this time as he was being inaugurated as president of a truly democratic South Africa on 10 May 1994.

Organising the inauguration was a logistical nightmare of massive proportions. Security was a sub-committee of the Inauguration Committee. It comprised officers of the old white apartheid regime and former members of *Umkhonto weSizwe* (MK), meaning 'Spear of the Nation', the ANC's military wing. An unlikely team, tasked with one of the toughest assignments ever: twelve days to co-ordinate the security of 184 heads of state or their representatives.

Although planning for the event had begun a year earlier, it was only after the April 1994 elections that the mainly black ANC security personnel became formally involved in the finer planning of the event. Keen not to be seen to be playing second fiddle, they were determined to stamp their authority on the occasion. And of course, they had their own rules when it came to Mandela's protection, rules that were firmly at odds with police protocol.

There were many clashes. And Steyn's contemptuous view was that they were simply being obstructive. But eventually the sheer proportions of the task forced everyone to put their differences aside, at least for the moment, and to concentrate on ensuring that the event ran smoothly.

It was an exercise on a scale the likes of which the South African Police had never before experienced. And they simply could not cope. Police officers who'd never done a day's work in VIP protection were called in. Desk workers and quartermasters alike were seconded to the operation.

Each head of state was assigned five officers and in some cases they were all complete novices. The assignment of teams to protect a range of leaders, from Fidel Castro and the Duke of Edinburgh to Hillary Clinton and Yasser Arafat, was a random exercise. Nine hundred officers were assembled on the Police College athletics field and assigned to the heads of state. The lack of experience showed. Determined not to let on that they were new to this, some over-zealous officers would jump out of cars, cock their assault rifles and adopt battle-stances as the door of a VIP car was opened. Clearly they'd watched just one American movie too many.

If that was not bad enough, the American Secret Service and the Israeli Mossad gave South Africa a really tough time with their often ridiculous requests. When it comes to security for their government representatives, Americans know only one method: the bigger, the better. In this case they were protecting US First Lady Hillary Clinton, Vice-President Al Gore and his wife, Tipper. They stood out like sore thumbs at the inauguration – the only three people in the massive crowd of dignitaries to be protected by bulletproof shields. In addition, the Americans besieged South Africa's VIP unit with their over-the-top demands. They insisted

on parking ambulances and communication vehicles behind the
Union Buildings and placing snipers on the turrets of the buildings.
These requests were all turned down. But then they simply went
their own way. Instead of sticking to the three-cars-five-protectors-
per-convoy rule, the Americans had ten cars in their convoy. And
not to be outdone, the Israelis went one better and had eleven.

Heads of state were to be collected from their hotels around
Gauteng, driven to Pretoria's Union Buildings and dropped off
there. Then the convoys would have to move on. All this had to
be co-ordinated on a minute-by-minute schedule. According to
international protocol, the order of arrivals starts with who's
been in power the longest. (Interesting to note that that's why
dictators tend to get first preference in state line-ups, simply by
virtue of the fact that they've held onto power for so long.)

As is the case with all carefully laid plans, things did not
always go according to schedule and eventually there was a massive traffic snarl-up. Britain's Prince Philip probably took the
most sensible route. He simply got out of his car and walked to
the venue. He would casually stop passers-by, ask for directions,
eventually surprising everyone by arriving at the VIP breakfast
on foot.

The Americans, of course, had to do their own thing regardless of how it affected everyone else. A one-way traffic system
had been specially designed for the event to avoid convoys clash-
ing with each other. The Americans decided that they were
above all this and took their convoy out of the traffic jam and
drove in on the 'out' route, incurring the wrath of 183 nations in
almost as many languages.

Most of the heads of state were staying in Johannesburg's
finest hotels. It was Rory Steyn's job to co-ordinate the hotel
security. Once all the heads of state had been dispatched to
Pretoria, Johannesburg became a ghost town and all that was left
for Steyn to do was put his feet up and watch the whole spectacle
on television.

It was a time of oddly conflicting emotions for this former
apartheid security officer. There were sworn communists like

Cuba's Fidel Castro, with Palestinian leader Yasser Arafat receiving rounds of applause nearly as loud as Mandela's. Then there was the deeply moving sight of a man who had spent 27 years in jail now reciting the oath of office, followed by what was to become a famous image of reconciliation as the new president held up high the hand of his former enemy – Deputy President De Klerk – and also that of the son of his long-time comrade, another Deputy President, Thabo Mbeki. And who could forget the gasps from the crowd as four South African Air Force Oryx helicopters flew over the Union Buildings carrying the new South African flag.

Steyn's head told him that South Africa was lost and that Mandela was going to sell them all down the river. But strangely his heart was saying something else; something that was only articulated when his father, who was also watching the inauguration on television, phoned and said to him: 'Well, my boy, what do you think?'

I think we're going to have to give the old man a chance, he replied. Little did Steyn know then that he would end up giving far more than a chance to this man he'd once regarded as evil incarnate.

And so began a battle for the heart and mind of Rory Steyn.

THE ROAD TO RECONCILIATION

Perhaps it all started with that wonderful moment at Johannesburg's Ellis Park Stadium on Inauguration Day, 1994. After a special inauguration lunch on 10 May, Mandela flew by helicopter to the stadium. In honour of this auspicious day, a special soccer match was played between South Africa and Zambia. At half time, with the score 0–0, Mandela walked onto the pitch to greet the teams. Half-time stretched into almost three-quarter time but nobody seemed to mind, so dizzy were they with the joy of this amazing moment. *Well, before we had returned to the presidential suite, which only took about five minutes, Bafana Bafana (as the South African team is fondly known) were suddenly 2–0 up. That's what I call a half-time team talk! It was true inspiration.*

Slowly the Madiba magic was being worked. Little did Steyn know then that it would take less than two months for Mandela to charm him onto his side.

Steyn was not promising material for reconciliatory change. Born to a typical, white, middle-class South African family, he grew up believing in the *swart gevaar* and Reds under the bed. The common family term for blacks was *kaffirs*, lazy, dirty criminals who threatened their Christian way of life. His paternal forefathers were Afrikaners who'd proudly been part of the Great Trek. However, his paternal grandfather and his father went to one of Cape Town's prestigious English-speaking boys' high schools. His mother was of direct English descent, and English was Steyn's home language. Although he regarded himself as an Englishman through-and-through, despite having an Afrikaans surname, he was not one of those English boys who had bought into the liberal mentality. He voted National Party until 1994 – a blinkered, white youth who hated blacks and regarded the outside world with suspicion.

On finishing school at Roosevelt High, Johannesburg, in 1981, he joined the South African Police Force. It was initially an indirect way to study law. His parents simply didn't have the money to send their teenage son to university. Law did not sit well with Steyn, however, so his next choice was teaching; but after the education administration lost his papers he decided he might as well remain in the police force as part of his obligatory military service for all white male school-leavers at that time. After all, there was a civil war to be fought and communist blacks were threatening South Africa's way of life!

Already identified early as one of the police's brightest young recruits, he was quickly targeted for the Security Branch. After doing a bit more studying, he was given his first special assignment. State President PW Botha had ordained that Special Investigation Units were to be set up with the exclusive task of interrogating high-profile anti-apartheid activists. This was initiated shortly before the 1986 State of Emergency. For six months Steyn served as a loyal member in a unit where intelligence work essentially involved detaining activists without trial, and interrogations meant torturing political detainees into submission.

He was getting deeper and deeper into the dark underbelly of a white racist state that would use any method to protect its *laager*. But fortunately for Steyn he was re-deployed after six months. It was this re-assignment that probably saved him from participating in the bloodier deeds of apartheid's dirty war. For there is no doubt that at that crucial stage in his career, he would have jumped at the chance to serve under somebody like Eugene de Kock (apartheid's number one assassin dubbed 'Prime Evil' and now serving a life prison sentence for murder and other gross human rights violations). Instead, Steyn was sent to the Security Branch's Churches Section, as his involvement in the church was well known. Moderate by comparison, here his job was to monitor radical Christian groups, listen to recordings of their tapped phones and, if necessary, engage in thuggish acts of harassment – such as ordering large quantities of sand to be dumped in the driveway of activists' homes in a bid to intimidate and frustrate them. He was only 22 at the time, very naïve and very flattered at being singled out at such a young age to do his bit for *volk en vaderland.*

In addition to these brutish acts, the Security Branch was also entrusted with another high-profile assignment – that of the protection of the country's prime ministers and state presidents. Brutally suppressing the majority of a country's people may bring with it a sense of absolute power, but it also brings with it absolute fear. White racist leaders were key targets and thus their safety was regarded as one of the most important jobs of the police force. In addition to the Security Branch, there was also the Special Guard Unit, whose job it was to see to the security of cabinet ministers, visiting heads of state, sports teams, and so on. In 1990 the Security Branch was restructured and renamed the Crime Intelligence Service; and Rory Steyn was given the task of heading up the VIP Protection Section.

On top of the restructuring, a whole new dynamic was introduced into the mix. Up until then, VIP protection (like every other state organ in apartheid South Africa) had been racially segregated. Even the high-risk job of being prepared to take a bullet for a revered apartheid leader was an honour reserved for whites only. Coloured and Indian officers saw to the protection of VIPs in their own racial groups serving in the Houses of Representatives and Delegates respectively, and a black major was responsible for the safety of black VIPs, essentially Bantustan leaders.

In 1992 the units became integrated. This was to be Steyn's first test. Up to this point, white officers had their own tea-room and toilets. To their horror they were now forced to share facilities with all races. The white members were up in arms, threatening to bring their own cups and not use the toilets at work. In the end, practicality triumphed over rigid ideology and, amazingly, the officers found that they could work together. Little did Steyn know that this would set the tone for a far more radical transformation under President Nelson Mandela.

A LESSON IN HUMILITY

Like all radical transformations, a dramatic change often begins with something small, almost inconsequential. For Steyn, there was no 'Road to Damascus' experience, no blinding flash of light. It began with the simplest and most basic of things: good manners! As a well brought up young white South African, common courtesy was very important to Steyn. He had certainly met his match in Mandela.

A product of his generation, chivalry was second nature to the President. He was a peculiar mix of a Victorian gentleman and African royalty. Steyn saw that he never walked past women or children without greeting them. Everyone was treated the same, irrespective of their colour, age, sex or social position. As he observed Mandela day in and day out for two months, he expected to see the cracks, but eventually Steyn was forced to the conclusion that the President was genuine: nobody could maintain a façade like that for so long. This, of course, was coupled with the man's speeches. As a presidential bodyguard,

Steyn listened to the President's public addresses over and over again. Relentlessly, Mandela would repeat his offer of reconciliation: 'Let's forget the past and together create a better future for all South Africans,' a message that was especially significant for this white officer who had a past he would sooner forget.

And in forgetting the past, there was also a very exciting future to look forward to. Mandela treated his protection unit very differently from what they were used to. For the first time, Steyn feels, *I was recognised as somebody, not a second-class citizen. When FW de Klerk became State President he didn't want any security personnel and really only tolerated them. President Mandela would always thank us, always acknowledge our presence. He made us feel that we were doing something vitally important for South Africa. And this really hit home hard. Here was I, this white racist who'd once wished Mandela had been sentenced to death. I thought, 'What does he owe me?' And yet there he was, this dignified old man, who treated me like an equal.* In fact, Mandela became so famous for greeting everyone wherever he went, from the most lowly to the highest, that even De Klerk was forced to follow his example.

There is a famous story among security personnel about De Klerk. As Mandela's deputy in post-apartheid South Africa, he also had his own contingent of security personnel. One day in Kimberly he decided to thank all the local officers who'd been specially brought in from that region to assist with his protection that day. Mistakenly, he shook hands with and thanked somebody who'd been working on his convoy for four years! De Klerk did not even know the faces, let alone the names of those who were willing to risk their lives for him.

This complete lack of regard for those working for him was nothing new. It was a hangover from South Africa's past. When the former National Party leaders were in power, their bodyguards and everybody else who worked in their households had strict instructions to stay out of sight when the State President was around. Not only could De Klerk not stand the fact that he had to have bodyguards wherever he went, but the status quo dictated that there were two classes of people – those who were waited upon and those who served. And the commanders made sure that the men understood this. They were literally told to make themselves invisible when he walked in and out of his house.

When Mandela became president, those who'd worked for De Klerk were amazed to find this new black leader not only regarding them as an integral part of his team but also going to the trouble to enquire after their well-being.

Initially, some of these white bodyguards would look for the nearest bush to hide behind when Mandela came out of his house. But slowly Mandela's charm and genuine friendliness drew them out of their shells. And in the end these bodyguards were among his most loyal followers, prepared to work the longest hours without so much as a murmur. All it took was a basic lesson in human relations. A lesson that Mandela was perfectly equipped to impart – for this, after all, was the essence of the man. He made it quite clear that he appreciated and accepted their vital role in ensuring the success of his presidency and their contribution to the new South Africa. How ironic that it should be a black man jailed for sabotage that would end up teaching these young men how to respect another human being as truly equal.

And this irony did not escape Steyn's attention. His friends and family pressurised him. 'What's it like working for Mandela?' they would ask, certain that Steyn would reveal what an ogre the President really was. Instead, he was eventually forced to admit that it was far nicer working for Mandela than it ever had been to work for De Klerk.

The day Madiba took office he was told about widespread fears among former Office of the State President's staff regarding their jobs. De Klerk had taken only a small component of staff, his inner core, with him to his new portfolio of second Executive Deputy-President. Whites left behind were left unbriefed in a great deal of confusion as to what their future held, as the precedent in the rest of Africa was to fire all the "colonial" government staff immediately.

Madiba called all the staff into the cabinet room. He said that the ANC had won the election and would run the country together with a government of national unity. He said that anyone who felt that they could not work together with the ANC should raise their hands. Those people would be allowed to leave and would receive their pension. Those who chose to stay however, would not lose their jobs. He said that the new government needed their experience and knowledge and asked them to train their new colleagues.

He wasn't finished. He spent the rest of the day going from office to office introducing himself. "What is your name? Where do you come from? How many children do you have?" etc. etc. By the time he was finished, Madiba had the most motivated staff with which any President had ever begun his term of office. One lady who had worked there for over 20 years told me that that was the first time any president ever came into her office!

THE REAL KHOTSO HOUSE STORY

By now Steyn was completely sold on Mandela, but it was the handling of the Khotso House debacle that committed him for life. When Steyn was implicated in the bombing of the South African Council of Churches (SACC) Headquarters *(see prologue),* he was called in and asked to explain his rôle to his superior, VIP Protection Director Gary Kruser. The fact that his name had been linked to the incident forced Kruser to take the matter up with the President as it could well mean that Steyn could be kicked out of the Presidential Protection Unit. This is what Steyn told Kruser and, later, Mandela himself.

In 1987 while working in the Security Branch's Churches Section, Steyn received an urgent call from the section head, Nannie Beyers. The Security Branch had an informer inside the Council of Churches who had leaked information that activist Wolfram Kistner – who had an office in the SACC headquarters at Khotso House – had received banned literature which was stored in his office. The plan was that if the Security Branch could find the material in his possession, Kistner could be arrested under South Africa's draconian security laws. *He was a real thorn in our flesh and we wanted him behind bars.* Beyers then planned a delicate operation in which he, together with Steyn and another colleague, Paul Erasmus, would enter Khotso House using a clandestine route that Beyers had discovered. All three men held the rank of warrant officer at the time, but Beyers was the senior of the trio and Steyn by far the most junior.

The operation took place under cover of darkness early one morning and involved climbing through a window of a block of flats adjacent to Khotso House and entering via a parking basement. *Beyers and I then pulled ourselves onto a landing which led to a fire escape and directly into Khotso House itself. Erasmus was too big and unfit – so he stayed downstairs in the basement and slashed the tyres of the SACC cars there just for fun.* Beyers and Steyn then moved straight to Kistner's office, tried the door and found that it was locked. *We left straight away without trying to get in. I think this was around 1 or 2 a.m. and we were only inside for a maximum of five minutes. All three of us left via the same route. We never pursued this thing about the documents again.*

Over a year later, on 31 August 1988, Khotso House hit the headlines. The building was blown to smithereens in a massive explosion in which 21 people were injured. *There was lots of whispering within John Vorster Square Security Branch after that. We all knew that the Security Branch Head Office was responsible, but no names were ever mentioned. Another rumour doing the rounds in the police corridors was that Law and Order Minister Adriaan Vlok was not happy that the job had taken so long to be done, as he had ordered it a long time ago.* Nevertheless, these views were never expressed publicly at the time and, in a blaze of publicity, Vlok falsely blamed the bombing on ANC activist Shirley Gunn (who later sued the Law and Order Minister).

Vlok subsequently told the Truth and Reconciliation Commission amnesty committee on 21 July 1998 that he had ordered the bombing under the direct instruction of State President PW Botha. The entire operation was carried out by Vlakplaas operatives, led by commander Eugene de Kock. The operation was handed over to De Kock after Johannesburg Security Branch operatives under the command of Charles Zeelie bungled the job. De Kock tells how he laughed when he heard that Zeelie had gone to Khotso House with a plastic bag full of limpet mines. The packet had burst, sending the contents rolling around the street. Needless to say, apartheid's number one assassin (who is serving a life sentence behind bars) completed the job to Vlok's specifications (and was finally granted amnesty for the bombing from the Truth and Reconciliation Commission in August 1999 during the writing of this book).

Meanwhile, Steyn only completed his bomb disposal and explosives training in 1989, a full year after the Khotso House affair. *By then I was an officer holding the rank of lieutenant and was no longer in the Churches Section.* Beyers remained in the unit while Erasmus was seconded to 'Stratcom' – a vicious intelligence unit that had as its aim the discrediting of the anti-apartheid United Democratic Front (UDF) and the ANC, using propaganda, lies and a series of other dirty tricks. Stratcom would perform illegitimate operations and then blame them on the UDF or ANC.

Beyers resigned from the police at the end of 1989 and Steyn never saw either him or Erasmus again, especially after he became VIP section head.

To Steyn's devastation, the Khotso House debacle returned to haunt him many years later. *Imagine my horror and acute embarrassment when a New Zealand photographer came up to me towards the end of the 1995 Rugby World Cup while I was protecting the All Blacks and asked me, 'Rory, is this you?'* He was referring to an exposé by journalist Stefaans Brümmer in the then *Weekly Mail*. Under the banner headline 'My Bag of Dirty Tricks', Paul Erasmus had given a tell-all account of his days in Stratcom, including what he describes as the final recce mission for the Khotso House bombing led "by Lieutenant Rory Steyn (now a major)".

Steyn was mortified as this had come as a complete surprise. His first thought was to consider legal action, but *a friend in the legal profession and former Johannesburg Security Branch member, Kingsley du Plessis, advised me against it saying that as soon as I went to the media and tried to defend my good name, I could end up implicating myself. It was good advice, but it did little at the time to soothe my anger.*

Since that article, Steyn has done a lot of soul-searching regarding Erasmus's motives for saying what he did. *There are three possibilities: either he was genuinely mistaken and not briefed properly that Beyers was in charge. Or he deliberately falsely implicated me in order to exonerate his friend, Beyers. (Erasmus never referred to Beyers by name in Brümmer's exposé and simply talked about 'another Security Branch member'.) Or he deliberately implicated me because he didn't like the fact that, although I was a lot more junior than him, I was promoted to lieutenant in 1987. Personally I think it was the third reason.*

Official police records confirm that Steyn only completed his bomb disposal and explosives training in 1989, long after Khotso House was blown up. And at no stage did he think that their 'trip' to the SACC headquarters was in fact a prelude to the bombing. He was firmly convinced at that time and for a long period afterwards, that they were going there to do exactly what Beyers intended – hunt for banned material in order to arrest Kistner. *With hindsight, however, I think I may have been a little naïve. I think there is a very real possibility that our 'mission' that night had nothing to do with Wolfram Kistner and his supposed subversive literature. I think it's more than likely that it was Beyers' way of testing the route into Khotso House and that he probably led De Kock and the Vlakplaas saboteurs into the building on the night of 31 August 1998.*

When Steyn was summoned by his superior, Gary Kruser, in 1996 to explain an intelligence report implicating him in the bombing of Khotso House, he explained all this. *But he told me that he would still have to take the matter to the President and I completely understood. If I had been in his shoes I would also not have wanted some former Security Branch member with Third Force allegations hanging over his head assigned to an icon like Nelson*

Mandela. And not just assigned, but in a senior position as the Team Leader of his personal protection team!

The rest is history. Steyn requested permission to speak to Mandela if he was to be dismissed. He in fact waited outside the President's office while Kruser spoke to him. *Obviously I do not know exactly what was said behind those closed doors, but I had a strong subconscious belief that I had done enough in the eight or nine months as President Mandela's Team Leader for him to clearly see my bona fides.* In fact Kruser now confirms that his intention in speaking to Mandela was to have Steyn removed from his post. He argued his case passionately, but to no avail. 'I tried to convince the President, but he was not interested. He told me, "This is a young boy. Why do you want to punish him? Why do you want to persecute him? I say he should not be removed from his post!" '

The final chapter in the Khotso House saga was written a year later during a heated parliamentary debate. Steyn was in Harare at the time preparing for a whistle-stop visit by Mandela. He was due to meet Zimbabwean President Robert Mugabe before flying off to the Botswana capital of Gaborone where he would brief Sir Ketumile Masire on certain SADEC developments. *I was watching SABC TV News in my room at the Harare Sheraton, when the newsreader announced, 'Today President Nelson Mandela hit back at National Party criticism of the government's affirmative action policy as "racism in reverse".* And then there was footage of Madiba speaking in parliament.* It was a dramatic moment and another example of Mandela's growing anger with De Klerk. Looking straight at his deputy, he sternly reprimanded him, 'You cannot say I am a racist. I have two *boeremeisies* (Afrikaans lasses) who work as my private secretaries, Elize Wessels and Zelda la Grange. The head of my security in Pretoria is a white major who was involved in the bombing of Khotso House. His bosses came to me and said he must be dismissed and I refused.' And then pointing at De Klerk, 'And if you don't believe me, you can come with me on my aeroplane to Pretoria and I'll call him.'

Steyn immediately telephoned his wife Gill and asked if she'd seen the news. She hadn't, so he quickly filled her in. *She was worried. I wasn't. I reckoned Madiba was making a good point!* But many other people had seen the news as the entire parliamentary debate was carried live around the globe by CNN. The next minute Steyn and his PPU colleagues were inundated with calls asking whether 'Rory had been fired.' Although Steyn was not concerned about this latest turn of events, he nevertheless thought that he should fill Mandela in on the exact details of what happened surrounding the Khotso House affair. *Upon my return to South Africa, I asked if I could see Madiba when we got to Houghton. I asked if I could explain the full story of what happened with the Khotso House bombing and I told him exactly what I had told Kruser and wrote in this book. He said, 'Oh, I see!' as if he was hearing this for the first time. All I can say is that my respect and admiration for him grew a thousandfold that day, because I realised that he had been willing to defend me and keep me on as his Team Leader, even though he firmly believed that I had been directly involved in the bombing. He could so easily have got rid of me. I was dispensable. But when it comes to reconciliation, small things are big things. I was completely sold on Nelson Mandela.*

A DIVIDED PROTECTION SQUAD UNITES

It was not, however, all smooth sailing. Steyn may have felt appreciated by his new boss, but there was another obstacle: overcoming the natural hostility of his new black counterparts in the unit. Once Mandela became president, the old white guard and the new black ANC security officers were forced to unite to form the new Presidential Protection Unit. It was a tenuous amalgamation of the ANC Department of Intelligence and Security (DIS) and MK personnel, together with white police VIP Protection Unit members. Both groups mistrusted each other and felt that if left alone they could do a much better job of protecting the President. As Kruser commented later, 'there were basically two units protecting Mandela.'

Not all attempts at uniting apartheid and ANC structures in the new South Africa have succeeded. But with Mandela there as a constant reminder, the possibility of successful change in the Presidential Protection Unit (PPU) was very real.

For the first twenty months of Mandela's term of office, Steyn co-ordinated his advance security in Johannesburg. But by 1996 the two units, the old apartheid structures and the MK units, had officially become one body. Steyn was offered the position as one of the team leaders on the PPU in January 1996. While an amalgamation might be easy to draft on paper, it is a different matter to ensure that it works effectively in practice.

Steyn knew that it was going to take time to earn the respect of both black and white colleagues. He already had a shining example in the President and knew that the only way to gain some kind of moral authority was to treat everyone equally. In the first two weeks the black members, represented by the second-in-command of the squad, came to Steyn with a list of grievances and what they perceived to be weaknesses in the structure. In the other camp were the old white officers who were carefully watching Steyn's every move. Some of them would try and influence him, whispering in his ear, 'Don't let them get away with this.' Throughout, Steyn stuck to one unwavering principle: 'Listen to everyone, show no favouritism.'

It all came to a head when one of the officers in the unit, Troy Irving, had an accident in Durban which resulted in a dent in Mandela's armoured BMW. The President was due to arrive the next day. It took a lot of organising behind the scenes, but Steyn ensured that the boot was replaced, resprayed and that a new bulletproof tyre and front fender (damaged by a blow-out *en route* from Johannesburg) were fitted – all this on a government petrol card with a R100 limit!

But the Afrikaans-speaking members of the unit were not happy. They were convinced that Steyn was covering up for his fellow Englishman. Departmental rules stipulate that police members are not liable for damage to government property if there is no negligence and the damage occurs during the execution of official duty. Steyn's attitude was that you always stand up for your team members – no matter who they are. He would always take their side unless, of course, there had been blatant misconduct and no sign of remorse. *This was one of the positive things that the Security Branch taught me.* But feelings were running high, and the matter had clearly become a cultural/racial issue, as black members were coming to Steyn and asking, 'What is this "Englishman-thing" we're hearing about?'

He called a team lunch meeting to explain his point of view. He decided to lay his cards on the table once and for all. He told them that he could not change the colour of his skin. To the whites he explained that he was the only ex-Security Branch member on the team and therefore had to prove to the ANC personnel that he was above suspicion and absolutely non-racist. To the blacks he said that he thought that he had done enough to prove his bona fides and now urgently needed their co-operation and support. Steyn's approach paid off and the lunch became a turning point for team relations. After this shared meal he was to enjoy universal support and frequent acknowledgement as one of the best team leaders on the Presidential Protection Unit.

Although members of the team were finally rallying around one another, they were still to face pressure from outside. Not only was Mandela head of the country, but prior to the end of 1997, he was also still president of the ANC. This entailed a weekly visit to the party's Johannesburg headquarters known then as Shell House. Mandela chose to spend every Monday morning at the party's offices dealing only with organisational matters. Initially, Steyn's visits to Shell House were not a pleasant experience. He had not been part of the struggle culture. In fact, the very opposite was true. And so it was that he would experience a feeling of foreboding come Monday mornings. He wondered if he would ever feel welcome in this environment. Every week he would meet key ANC figures, people he'd grown up believing were communist terrorists who, if given half a chance, would have slit his throat under apartheid rule. And every week, instead of hostility, he encountered only friendliness from virtually every senior ANC representative in that office. Once again he was experiencing democracy first hand. Here he was not regarded as a second-class citizen, despite his background. Here he was treated as somebody special, somebody doing a service for the President. *I have to single out Aziz Pahad here – an SACP member and someone I was brought up to believe was the Devil incarnate. Whenever he was around he would come up to us with a smile as wide as Muizenberg beach and greet us. He never walked past us without a friendly greeting and a chirp!*

But although he felt his acceptability growing in his job, there was still a lot of sensitivity around Mandela's protection in the early days of his presidency. The ANC wasn't entirely convinced that everyone (particularly the former apartheid guards) had Mandela's best interests at heart. So initially the unit went to great lengths to ensure that there was always a racially mixed team accompanying Mandela. There came a day, however, when this simply wasn't possible. The President visited Shell House one Saturday morning to attend to a National Executive Committee (NEC) meeting. He planned to leave at midday to host a special lunch at his Houghton home for the former president of Tanzania, the late Julius Nyerere.

He told his bodyguards that he wouldn't be needing them after the lunch, as he planned to stay at Houghton for the rest of the day. A separate component of uniformed police officers was employed to watch the house and a smaller group from within the team would remain on stand-by in case of emergencies. The team was divided into four groups for these stand-by duties. These groups within the team were arranged geographically to ensure a good response time, in that each smaller group took home one of the police cars in case of an emergency.

Steyn dismissed his men for the rest of the day, but not before reminding them that they were on stand-by as usual. He stayed behind at Houghton with three other white protection officers.

Glad for some time off from their busy schedules, most of the black members went off to Ellis Park where a soccer match was being played. But it so happened that Mandela changed his mind after lunch and decided that he needed to go back to Shell House after all. Steyn immediately activated the other members of the team, but could not get hold of those watching the soccer game. The net result was that they arrived at Shell House with an all-white team, apart from one Indian member, Ashwyn Govind, much to the annoyance of ANC security. A huge issue was made of it and the matter was reported to ANC spokesman, Ronnie Mamoepa, and Deputy Minister of Intelligence, Joe Nhlanhla, both NEC members. But when Steyn was finally able to discuss the matter with the President at the end of the day's work, Mandela only laughed, unable to understand what all the fuss was about. He trusted his men equally, but promised to raise the matter with Nhlanhla.

However, at the next day's team briefing, the issue was raised by the bodyguards themselves, who declared that they were sick and tired of this 'black and white' thing and 'would take issue with anyone who made a big deal of it.' To his credit, Steyn's then national commander, Jason Tshabalala (a former MK soldier), took the issue up personally with ANC security, saying they were never to be so petty again. A seemingly minor incident, in retrospect, but one that would result in lasting friendships. In particular, Steyn found himself opening up to Tshabalala and other black members of his team.

And if anyone doubted the power of Mandela's message of reconciliation, they would only have to witness the transformation of this once-divided PPU. All of this was given greater impetus by the changing political climate around them.

The backdrop was the Truth and Reconciliation Commission. One by one, victims of abuse were coming forward to share their stories of apartheid's atrocities and one by one the faceless perpetrators of this terror began confessing their brutal past. For Steyn this was a real eye-opener.

There was one particular story that struck very close to home. Despite the release of Mandela from jail, 1991 was still a very turbulent time for South Africa. Steyn was sitting in his office on the 9th floor of the notorious John Vorster Square

(Johannesburg's largest police station) when the phone rang with his commanding officer Colonel Neels van Wyk on the line: 'Rory, there's a limpet mine attached to a car just outside the main entrance of the station.' Steyn was by then trained in bomb disposal and he was ideally placed to assist in this emergency. He had been instrumental in de-activating a similar limpet mine at a Shell garage a few weeks earlier.

This particular type of limpet mine had been one of the weapons of choice of the liberation armies in South Africa. Although it only contained around one kilogram of explosives, aluminium powder in the explosives mixture burned at over 6 000 °C during detonation, causing a huge fireball. Anyone in the vicinity not killed by the explosion was in danger of being killed by inhaling this fireball.

Steyn rushed downstairs. He knew that he didn't have much time. He grabbed the limpet mine off the car it was attached to, unscrewed the detonator and threw it as far away as possible. This was not the correct way to diffuse it, but there was no time to put on a bomb-disposal suit, as it was a few minutes before 7:30 a.m. and large numbers of people were on their way to work.

The gamble paid off and he was able to destroy the detonator in a controlled explosion. But Steyn knew that he and hundreds of others in that busy area had come very close to death.

His brave deed was rewarded with a letter of commendation from the apartheid government's Minister of Law and Order, Adriaan Vlok. He had already been awarded the South African Police Star for Combating Terrorism.

Six years later, however, it emerged at a Truth and Reconciliation Commission hearing that the Shell garage and John Vorster Square limpet mines had been deliberately planted by apartheid agents based at Vlakplaas. The timing of the first coincided with Shell's refusal to disinvest in South Africa and this 'Stratcom' operation was planned to discredit the ANC, making it look as if they had not yet embraced peace and were still busy planting bombs. Steyn felt sick when he realised that it was white people (his own so-called colleagues) who had done this, simply to discredit the ANC. Those explosions could have left his wife a widow and killed scores of innocent people. He began to ask himself the question, 'Who are the real terrorists?'

Months later he told Jason Tshabalala this story while chatting at the PPU offices. He threw the medal he had received out of the first floor window. *I felt totally embarrassed and disgraced that I had proudly worn that medal on my wedding day. I have never worn it since.*

It was moments like these that cemented unity within the Presidential Protection Unit. And of course in addition to these personal chats, taking pride in a job well done is always a great morale booster for any team. When the group first started working as a team, not everyone had the same level of training, so everyone had different ideas about what their role was. As part of their in-service training, Steyn attempted to standardise a unique operating procedure. Working over and over again on their convoy positions and foot formations, they eventually developed a routine operating method. *I want to state without reservation that although we didn't have the budget of the United States Secret Service or the educational level of the British Metropolitan Police, I will back our guys against anybody in the world when it comes to crowd control and protecting a president in such a situation. The public appeal of President Mandela has made it essential that our formation be on top of their game and each individual member had to know exactly where he or she fitted in and what his or her job was. It was always a source of pride to me when I saw my team go into action and successfully negotiate another operation. To an outsider it might have looked like a bunch of bodyguards in black suits and dark glasses surrounding Madiba, but I say that my guys did a superb job and had what it takes to compete anywhere in the world.*

The more the teams were successful in their work together, the more lasting bonds were formed. And it wasn't always hard work. The long hours, the constant travelling and time spent away from home in each other's company in preparation for a trip meant that the team members got to know each other pretty well. *One particular aspect of the job I knew I'd miss was the advance missions to other provinces. Going to Durban was particular fun. There's something exciting about meeting at Houghton at five in the morning when it's still dark, then leaving together in a convoy. We always stopped at the same little coffee shop in Harrismith for breakfast. We filled up (the cars and ourselves) and by then the staff there knew us pretty well.* The group would always attract a bit of attention, as even in the new South Africa they were still an unusual sight, this mixed group of black and white bodyguards sitting together like old mates, chatting and eating their food. *If we'd get a free morning while down in Durban we would make our 'base-camp' the Wimpy on the city's Main Beach. Here we would spend the time swimming and body-surfing. There was a real sense of camaraderie on these trips and it was always good to get away together.*

RECONCILIATION MADIBA STYLE

The change that occurred in Steyn was starting to happen around South Africa as well. There would still be many whites unable to ask for forgiveness from black South Africans and others who would simply emigrate. Even in the face of this resistance, Mandela continued to display an extraordinary generosity of spirit.

It is now a well-established fact that Mandela's presidency was characterised by a remarkable period of reconciliation in South Africa. *I believe that that is what Madiba was destined for.*

Later during his term of office Mandela was sometimes criticised by members of his own party who felt that the President was too soft on those white South Africans who refused to embrace the new South Africa and yet benefited significantly from the changes in the country. Mandela was accused of favouring whites at the expense of ensuring social transformation of the lives and conditions of black South Africans. However, nothing could be further from the truth. And no doubt the history books will reflect that far from 'selling out', Mandela was a true peacemaker. His actions came at a time in the country when reconciliation was critical if bloodshed was to

be averted. It was a reconciliation that embraced people across
the political spectrum from white to black, right to left. People
quickly forgot that prior to the miracle of the 1994 elections,
parts of the country were engaged in bloody violence. Racist
white Afrikaners were threatening civil war, and to prove their
point planted several bombs just days before the first non-racial
poll, while in some black townships apartheid hit squads were
fuelling violence between the ANC and the Inkatha Freedom
Party. The so-called 'Third Force' continued well after the 1994
elections, resulting in many a bloody massacre before the fragile
peace that emerged towards the end of 1998.

It is against this backdrop that Mandela's reconciliatory presidency must be seen. A backdrop which, if properly understood,
not only shows just how radical the President's actions were but
how visionary, how desperately necessary for a peaceful transi-
tion to democracy.

AMABOKOBOKO!

The examples of reconciliation are many. On a grand scale there
was the 1995 Rugby World Cup tournament held in South Africa.
One simple gesture would turn out to be one of the most politically potent statements Mandela would ever make and arguably
the defining moment of his policy of reconciliation.

Rugby, as South Africa knows only too well, had an ugly history in this country. It had long been considered to be an
apartheid sport, the domain of racist white Afrikaners.
Throughout National Party rule it remained largely a 'whites
only' sport, but for this there was a price to pay. International
sanctions against South Africa included sport within the ambit
of the 'cultural boycott' and so the country's rugby
players were prevented from testing their skills against the best
in the world. It was a sore point with rugby supporters and the
government attempted to defy the sports embargo by organising
'rebel tours' to South Africa in the 1980s. These almost always
turned ugly as thousands of anti-apartheid activists would
organise protests around the illegal games. And when the

protests ended in chaos with police intervention, it only served to highlight the brutally oppressive nature of a police state.

It's no wonder that even after Mandela came to power, rugby and its supporters were treated with suspicion by most black people. And the fact that dyed-in-the-wool racists would still take the old South African flag to matches and refuse to sing the new national anthem did nothing to encourage a less antagonistic view towards the sport and its supporters.

Nevertheless, in the spirit of the new South Africa, the 1995 Rugby World Cup tournament was held in South Africa. And to everyone's surprise, the South African team – led by its now legendary captain, Francois Pienaar – made it to the final. Slowly the unity that sport brings was casting its glow over South Africa. Black South Africans, who, for the most part, were generally more interested in soccer than rugby and who understood little about the game, started taking pride in the fact that 'their team' was doing so well. Thus far this had all been encouraged by Mandela himself, who was there to support the team's (and the tournament's) opening match. It was played against the World Cup holders Australia, and throughout the game Mandela sat next to the Australian Prime Minister, Paul Keating. He got so caught up in the game that he would excitedly punch the Prime Minister on the arm every time South Africa scored. But the *pièce de résistance* was still to come.

Two days before the final was to be played at Johannesburg's Ellis Park Stadium, Mandela asked the South African team if he could have one of their rugby jerseys. Captain Francois Pienaar brought his own personal jersey, the one that he had worn in the opening match at Newlands, to the President, thinking that Mandela just wanted it for sentimental reasons. He certainly never imagined the sequence of events that would follow.

Mandela wanted to make a statement. He wanted the country to know that this rugby team was now welcome in the new South Africa and worthy of the support of all South Africans. It's important to point out that the springbok emblem was seen by many black South Africans as one of the most potent symbols of apartheid. And, in fact, the thinking at the time of the Rugby World Cup was that the springbok as an emblem should be scrapped. There was no place for an outdated and repressive symbol in the new South Africa. It was an extremely emotional and sensitive issue.

And so when Mandela arrived at Ellis Park Stadium on the day of the final, 24 June 1995, wearing the Springbok rugby jersey, complete with his trademark top button done up and waving a Springbok cap, he was making one of the most powerful statements of his career. It was not without its critics. His own political party and constituency did not support the retention of the springbok as rugby's emblem and his decision to don the Springbok jersey went against the advice of all his advisers and many senior members of the ANC. But his unique political insight proved to be spot on, because in that moment when he walked into the stadium wearing the jersey, he did more to win disgruntled white South Africans onto his side than any speech could ever hope to achieve.

'First he went to the presidential suite and chatted to rugby boss Dr Louis Luyt. Then he went to the changing rooms to speak to the team. Well, Francois nearly flipped when he saw Mandela wearing his jersey! He never thought this would happen,' remembers Des van Rooyen, the PPU planning officer for the final. Then Mandela went out onto the pitch waving at the crowd. 'Well, that just did it! The whole crowd went mad, chanting in unison: "Nelson, Nelson!" The President then greeted each team, and the atmosphere was electric. There was no way South Africa could lose after that. They were playing on sheer adrenalin.'

All Black legend and captain of New Zealand on that day, Sean Fitzpatrick, said, 'The power of a new united South Africa took us all by surprise. The influence that the appearance of Mandela had on the final was enormous.' François Pienaar, in his 1999 autobiography *Rainbow Warrior,* writes, "Shivers went up and down my spine. I could feel the country changing – eyes being opened, hearts being won, long-held prejudices being exposed."

When the final whistle blew, Luyt and Mandela hugged each other. In a few moments Mandela would hand the Webb Ellis Cup to Pienaar, victoriously clenching his fists above his beaming face. This would elicit those immortal words from Pienaar when asked on the podium what it felt like to win the World Cup in front of 63 thousand people: 'Not 63 thousand, but 42 million people!'

Meanwhile, outside the stadium, black South Africans gathered in their numbers, chanting *'Amabokoboko!'* and dancing in the streets with their deliriously happy white compatriots. It was even better than inauguration day. The whole country came together as one, all differences forgotten, united in their common joy that South Africa were world champions. Unfortunately the World Cup elation did not last. Rugby was to go through some serious knocks ending in an ugly court case. The sport simply refused to change its all-white hue and was exceptionally slow in kicking off its development programmes in black communities. Later in his presidency, Mandela ordered an inquiry into the administration of the sport following allegations of corruption and nepotism against Louis Luyt. Stubborn to the end, Luyt took the unprecedented move of challenging the inquiry in a court of law and subpoenaing the President to the proceedings. When Mandela stood up to take the oath at that court case, it was probably one of rugby's lowest moments ever. It was as if all the good work surrounding the World Cup was erased in a single moment. It was an assault on the President's dignity. Luyt won the battle, but lost the war and was eventually forced to resign as rugby's chief administrator.

The dramatic court case had been preceded by another dirty incident of racism as well. By 1996, Francois Pienaar had been replaced as captain and coach Kitch Christie's tenure as national coach had ended. In his place, André Markgraaff was given the responsibility of coaching the Springboks. Privately expressed sentiments had erupted and a bitter row over the lack of black representation in the South African side ensued. Markgraaff had stubbornly refused to consider the matter, but the final blow came when he was recorded during a private conversation describing South African Rugby Football Union (SARFU) Vice-President Mluleki George as a *kaffir*.

In a blaze of controversy, Markgraaff was forced to resign. And whatever gains the sport had made during the 1995 Rugby World Cup fever had not only been lost, but rugby had in fact taken several steps backward. *I regard this failure to capitalise on a unique opportunity of nation building as the single saddest aspect of our new South Africa. A ripe plum that was never picked, but rather left to rot. So sad.*

Markgraaff's privately expressed racism captured so dramatically on tape confirmed what most black people secretly thought went on behind the closed doors of many a white family. The sport was so badly damaged that, still to this day, it has not managed to fully recover the national support it had attained in one single day on 24 June 1995. Perhaps it never will. *This is also not helped by the behaviour of many white rugby supporters today. I find it inconceivable that the majority of whites still can't sing our new national anthem. They should ask their kids to teach them, as they all learn it at school, English and Afrikaans speaking. And I detest the waving of the old flag. It's high time that we as the majority rugby supporters sort this out ourselves. A little bit of vigilantism is, in this instance, not a bad thing!*

But on a personal level, Mandela still found it in himself to make amends with Markgraaff. It occurred at the beginning of 1999 at a foreign policy workshop just outside Johannesburg.

Every year the Department of Foreign Affairs recalls all its ambassadors and high commissioners for a week-long workshop. The purpose is mainly to spell out major foreign policy changes. In 1999 it took place at a hotel in Vanderbijlpark and was to be addressed by the President himself. On arrival, the PPU advance team led by Steyn bumped into the CATS Super 12 rugby squad that now had the formerly disgraced Markgraaff as its coach (his re-entry to rugby following the tape scandal). It was not surprising that the bodyguards saw Markgraaff at breakfast that morning. Steyn went over to him and informed him that Mandela would be arriving shortly and might ask to see him. Steyn was already aware that Markgraaff had written Mandela a letter the previous year apologising for the racist incident to the President personally. He also explained why he was resigning as the Springbok coach. Mandela had told Steyn about this letter one day at his residence in Houghton.

When Mandela arrived, Steyn informed him that Markgraaff was there and, true to form, the President expressed an interest in seeing him. Upon entering the lobby the President as usual was mobbed by the hotel staff, fans and the rugby team. After shaking hands with all of them he asked in Afrikaans, *'Waar's André?'* (Where's André?). The coach appeared and the two men shook hands publicly with the President commenting on the good work that Markgraaff was doing with Griqualand West and the CATS.

After addressing the Foreign Affairs workshop, he then told Steyn to go and fetch Markgraaff. *The President spent about ten minutes with him behind closed doors and then came out with his hand on Markgraaff's shoulder. Another magnanimous gesture of putting the past behind. Markgraaff was very grateful and wrote me a personal note. I felt proud to have contributed to this small gesture of reconciliation. Although I still wish rugby hadn't blown it so badly.* In fact this was not the only time that Steyn and some of Mandela's other senior bodyguards would assist the President in keeping up to date in the arena of South African sport. Steyn, being a rugby and cricket fan, would regularly inform the President of developments in these and other sports and personal matters regarding the teams' players as well. And so Mandela got to congratulate Pienaar on the birth of his baby in London while Pienaar was player/manager of Saracens, and to phone and congratulate Daryll Cullinan on his SA Test record of 275 not out.

And on another occasion at Steyn's prompting, he invited the Bok captain Gary Teichmann, coach Nick Mallett and manager Arthob Pietersen for lunch after the success of the 1997 European tour. This support for the country's sporting stars spread across the spectrum and included soccer, cricket, golf, boxing and athletics, to name but a few. Mandela would often phone teams and individuals before a match to wish them good luck and, without fail, speak to them after a game, tournament or race to congratulate them on their achievements. And while wearing the Springbok jersey became a defining moment for Mandela, he was always fair and followed this up by wearing the colours of South Africa's soccer squad, *Bafana Bafana,* during their victory at the African Cup of Nations in 1996, and also the South African Cricket Squad's obliteration of England in the one-day series in 1995/1996. It seemed that whenever Mandela wore the colours of a sporting code, the team would win. It was this fact that gave rise to the phrase 'Madiba Magic'.

However, the effort that went into casting this spell was not always straightforward. On the occasion that Mandela wore the cricket blazer and tie given to him by cricket captain Hansie Cronjé, he decided that he needed a pair of cricket whites (trousers) and shoes to match. *Needless to say he caused absolute pandemonium when he went to Sandton City's Total Sports to purchase them. The sports shop was forced to close its doors to customers. And in the end said that they would have the pair of trousers tailored for the President. These were ready the next day and the bodyguards fetched them, rather than Madiba causing chaos again.*

But if the truth be told, although Mandela has invested a lot of energy in promoting reconciliation through sport, he's actually not that keen on it. He doesn't like going to live matches, which he explains as being a result of the fact that he can't stand the tension. *I think it's that he thinks his time can be better spent. When he does go, it's more for the symbolism than because he enjoys the game.*

EXTENDING A HAND OF FRIENDSHIP TO THE ENEMY

Throughout his presidency Mandela became famous for the hand of reconciliation he offered to white Afrikaners. The President had had plenty of practice. During his 27 years in prison he had charmed many a white Afrikaner and developed a lasting friendship with one of the prison warders assigned to him. In 1994 he took the unusual step of visiting Betsie Verwoerd, widow of apartheid's architect Hendrik Verwoerd. The meeting took place in Orania, a small white enclave in the heart of Afrikanerdom. This community is unable to adapt to the new South Africa and so has taken itself into this remote rural area and seeks to build a community based entirely on white supremacy. Blacks are not allowed to live or work there and everything is done by whites. The community leaders might have fooled themselves that they were living in white utopia, but when the President decided to visit the area, they could hardly say no. After all, although this racist set-up was tolerated in South Africa, the land was not legally theirs to segregate.

The visit came about after Mandela had invited a number of South Africa's veteran women for tea at his presidential residence in Pretoria. All the wives of the former apartheid presidents were there as well as ANC stalwarts such as Adelaide Tambo and Albertina Sisulu. However, although the 94-year-old Betsie Verwoerd was invited, she was not well enough to attend. So when Mandela was told this by Elize Botha (wife of PW), he announced that if Betsie Verwoerd was not well enough to visit him, he would go and see her for tea. The President was confident that it would be a success despite a number of raised eyebrows from among his staff and colleagues. It was now time to test one of the toughest of all his opponents, Betsie Verwoerd.

PPU protector Johan Scott was dispatched to do the advance work on the trip, as he was a true Afrikaner who at least stood a chance of being accepted by the people of Orania. He met with the town fathers and informed them that the President would be stopping by. Their response was that Mandela would be allowed into the village, but he could not bring any black bodyguards or police officers with him. Bluntly Scotty told them that he would be returning to Pretoria and requesting police assistance, not specifically white or black policemen, but just police officers. Their response was, 'All right, they can come, but just ensure that the black policemen are at least accompanied by white policemen.' In the end there were probably more black people in Orania on the day of the visit than whites. Mandela was accompanied by a massive media contingent comprising all races and there really wasn't a thing the town fathers could do about it.

Mandela arrived with his team of black and white bodyguards and this equally mixed group of journalists in tow. He sat down to tea with Betsie Verwoerd, whose only comment afterwards was that Mandela was a real gentleman. No doubt her late husband would have been turning in his grave. But in the end everything worked extremely well. 'And all those rightwingers who'd been complaining and making such a noise,' remarks Scotty, 'were falling over themselves, trying to shake Madiba's hand and have photographs taken with him. Such is the impact of the man!'

This kind of gesture was also not simply a one-off, publicity-motivated event. Mandela was to display a unique level of consistency once he had decided that this was the route he would follow. The Orania tea was to have a sequel early in 1996 when he invited a delegation of Afrikaner women who had written to him expressing certain concerns to his residence in Pretoria: Mahlamba Ndlopfu. During this occasion he'd laboured through a carefully prepared speech in Afrikaans, in which he assured the group that they, as Afrikaners and women, had a role to play in South Africa, and even more importantly, that this was their country and that their language was safe. *He completely stole their hearts, behaving like the perfect gentleman that he is. I remember one of them even commenting that it was surprising how, in the new South Africa, one could gain such direct access to the President when it wasn't always possible under the old regime.*

SIMPLE ACTS OF KINDNESS

Both the Rugby World Cup and the Orania visits were high-profile media events that attracted nationwide and international attention. But it was not done only for the media. And evidence of this is that there were many humble examples of reconciliation that would become Mandela's trademark – simple acts of kindness that portrayed the measure of this great man. And simple acts that didn't always make it into the public eye, or at least not until well after the event had taken place.

There is the story of the 13-year-old Jewish boy who wanted to invite Mandela to his bar mitzvah. His parents explained that it was a futile hope. The President was a busy man and couldn't be bothered with this small, relatively insignificant social occasion. But the child would not take no for an answer and eventually persuaded his grandfather to drive him around to Mandela's Houghton residence where he handed over an invitation to the uniformed police officer at the gate. His parents heard about this and braced themselves for their child's disappointment when Mandela would obviously not appear on the big day. To their absolute amazement, a few days later Mandela phoned them personally to find out their address and inform the boy that he would be attending. And attend he did! It was the happiest day of that young boy's life. This was quickly followed by a plethora of similar invitations, just too many functions for the President to attend and so he was forced to decline. But his point had been made. He was not too important or too grand to attend to the smallest of details, despite his demanding schedule.

There were of course other equally charming examples. The President's bodyguards found themselves living this somewhat bizarre, split existence. Sometimes they would find themselves being fêted in the grandest of hotels, palaces or presidential guest-houses as Mandela toured the world. And then just a few days later, they would find themselves working a lonely night-shift, or preparing the advance work in a small town where the President was scheduled to visit a young child, stop over in a hospital or tour a poverty-stricken village.

There was the time Mandela flew up to Secunda in Mpumalanga, to visit an 11-year-old girl dying of a terminal disease. It was literally her dying wish to meet the President. It was granted!

DANGEROUS RECONCILIATION

Practising reconciliation was not always that simple either. There were a number of occasions when the President's desire for unity and peace brought about some personal risk. In most cases, these incidents happened in the volatile KwaZulu-Natal province, where Third Force-fuelled violence between the ANC and the IFP had raged on for over a decade. Townships became battle zones with clearly demarcated areas in which opposing political factions entered at their own risk. In March 1996 there was much talk of having a peace *imbizo* in KwaZulu-Natal to discuss the relentless violence. Zulu King Goodwill Zwelethini hosted what was known as a pre-*imbizo*, to plan for the actual meeting. It was held at the king's headquarters in Nongoma, the Zulu heartland where many people supported IFP leader Mangosuthu Buthelezi. A huge crowd of IFP representatives as well as chiefs, headmen and traditional leaders attended this meeting. But there was tension in the air and the royalty protection guards and PPU advance team were forced to confiscate a huge pile of 'traditional weapons' that included assegais, knives, *knopkieries* and axes, prior to the start of the peace talks.

Mandela addressed the crowd in Zulu, but it did not go down all that well, and at one point members of the crowd started shouting *'Hamba! Hamba!'* (Go away!) *Things were steadily becoming more tense. At one point I considered evacuating the President. Certainly we would have taken him out of there if the mounting tension grew worse, but fortunately it didn't. We had positioned a police armoured personnel carrier, a Nyala, right behind the marquee in which the meeting was held. I was already gripping a knife in my hand that I planned to use to slit the canvas and evacuate him straight to the Nyala if necessary.*

There was another occasion in KwaZulu-Natal where the presidential bodyguards became a bit worried. Mandela was in the area campaigning for local government elections in June 1996. The local government elections had already been postponed in this region due to the violence and tension in some parts of the community. On this particular occasion the presidential party accompanied by local ANC leader, now Deputy President, Jacob Zuma was running late. They still had one more stop at a hostel in the black township of Claremont. And Steyn was growing concerned. *It was getting dark, we had been at it the whole day and I suggested to Madiba that we rather not go. I explained that it was dark and that KwaZulu-Natal was not a safe place, particularly after night fell. And President Mandela was bound to have his detractors as well as supporters in this volatile region.* The helicopter pilot transporting Mandela from one area to the next was also worried. He didn't like the idea of taking off with Mandela in the dark. *Madiba listened (he would always listen to things that made sense), but then carefully explained that people had been told that he'd be coming and if he didn't pitch, it would create more problems. Those who said that "Mandela was coming" and had organised the programme, risked being killed for lying if he didn't turn up. I immediately saw that this was no exaggeration and we were forced to go in.*

We were careful to surround the President with bodyguards and left immediately when the visit was over. Fortunately everything went smoothly, but there were often moments like this when Madiba contravened international security standards in pursuit of a greater good.

This pursuit of the greater good not only threatened the President's personal safety, but on a few frightening occasions put him in the direct line of fire. Perhaps the most serious of these was just prior to the 1994 elections. Mandela was not yet president and thus not eligible for state bodyguards. He was therefore forced to rely on his own ANC security, who, while being experts in their field, were not as well resourced as their government counterparts.

These ANC bodyguards travelled the length and breadth of the country with Mandela, campaigning for the upcoming election. Now in those days, Northern Natal was a war zone and in particular the Inkatha Freedom Party stronghold of Naledi had become a no-go zone for ANC members. The ANC had all but been kicked out of the township and most of their houses had been burnt down by rival IFP members. The very popular Communist Party leader, the late Chris Hani, had tried to enter the area and had been prevented from doing so. Even ANC firebrand Winnie Madikizela-Mandela had been unable to set foot there. But Mandela was determined that he would succeed in going where no one else had gone before. He felt that it was critical for a future president to show that he was a leader for all the people and not just his own political party. The designated security members went to the local police for assistance, but as Mandela was not their boss yet, they were under no obligation to provide help. They informed the ANC that they were simply not prepared to enter this township with ANC leaders, as it was 'too dangerous'.

The verdict then from the ANC bodyguards was that it was just not safe for Mandela to go there. They briefed their president and other senior ANC members accordingly. But from the President down, they were all insistent that they could not be intimidated. Mandela called the then ANC head of security and later Head of the National Protection Service, Gary Kruser, aside and said to him, 'Look, I am going in there. Your job is to protect me, not to tell me what to do.' This comment was to become a mantra among future bodyguards whenever they tried to prevent Mandela from doing something they considered reckless. But despite the orders from above, the security detail was quite upset, as they knew they simply did not have adequate resources. Using every means possible, they managed to get a supply of AK-47s from their underground structures. They then sent their local men into the area on a recce, only to be told that they too would not dare cross the border into this war zone.

So when the designated day dawned, the contingent moved in, having had no advance tour of the area. They were literally entering the unknown. Speaking many years later on 702 Talk Radio, Kruser says, 'It was literally the only time in my life that I was in a black township with Mandela and not a single person came out into the streets to greet him. People were terrified, peeping through their windows and hiding in their houses. Within two or three minutes gunshots were going off everywhere. It was very frightening. I instructed my colleagues to take out their AK-47s in a show of strength and I ordered them to surround Mandela.' This meant that the other ANC executive members were left without protection. 'But,' says Kruser, 'I didn't care. We had one responsibility there and that was Mandela. I was determined that we would throw all our resources around him. But soon enough the other ANC members started complaining – the very ones who had been so insistent that we go into this township. I told them, 'You wanted to come and see the burnt-out houses. We are going to look at every single one.' But in reality I wasn't sure we would come out of there alive.' Needless to say they did live to see another day. And sure enough the next day at a rally in the same province, Mandela was boasting that they'd entered a no-go zone, saying that those who wanted to use home-made guns against him, had better be careful as they were pitted against the sophisticated weaponry of his bodyguards!

" . . .

An allegory told by
Nelson Mandela

There was a young man who decided to travel the world in search of the wife of his dreams. In doing so, he crossed vast plains, mighty rivers and the highest mountains. He courted beauty queens, princesses and many rich and famous women. He could not, however, find the woman of his dreams. Devastated, he returned to his country and prepared to live a lonely life there until his death. He finally arrived at the village of his birth. Upon entering the village he met a girl from next door. They were of the same age, had gone to school together and had danced together. Immediately it struck him that this was the girl he had been seeking his whole life.

. . . "

.

2

The People's President

'Smile, when you push the people.'

I t is believed that bodyguards entrusted with the job of ensuring the safety of a head of state often take on the characteristics of the person they are protecting. And this was a belief Rory Steyn was to see put into practice over and over again during his travels around the world with Mandela.

Everywhere, the people – the security personnel and those around the leader – start acting like him or her.

Mandela's security team was a perfect example of this. There was a standing joke among his bodyguards that began when Mandela first came into office. Whenever large crowds surrounded the President, his unit immediately moved into a special formation around him. Each person in this formation had a specific job. The number one bodyguard walked right behind the President. He didn't worry about the crowds; he had only one concern – never to take his eyes off his leader. This was usually an experienced officer who was also fairly tall. He would be somebody the President was familiar with, as he would have to travel in the car with Mandela. Now travelling with Mandela was a little like moving around with an international pop star.

Everywhere he went he was mobbed by huge crowds eager to shake hands or just catch a glimpse of this world-famous leader. Often the bodyguards were called upon to push the crowds back so that they didn't pose a threat to the President's or their own safety. (The President's car was armoured and weighed over three tons.)

The bodyguards had a hard time because Mandela liked talking to and meeting people and would often willingly walk straight into potentially dangerous situations.

The same thing happened when the President got into his car. Crowds pushed up against the vehicle in the misguided hope that the President would see them, roll down the car windows and greet them. Again in situations like these where there was great confusion and chaos, the bodyguards were called upon to push the crowds back. When the President first saw this happening, he turned to the number one bodyguard sitting in the car with him and said 'Please, tell your chaps to smile when they push the people!' And ever after, every time there was a potential confrontation between security and over-eager crowds, Mandela repeated this phrase, 'Please, tell your chaps to smile when they push the people.'

At other times it would be the media that was on the receiving end of the President's generosity of spirit. The media and presidential security were natural adversaries. The media's job was to get as close to the President as possible just in case there was a choice soundbite in the offing. The Presidential Protection Unit's responsibility was to keep potential troublemakers as far away from the President as possible. Often the bodyguards would quite forcibly push the press away. And equally often the President would see this and shout out, 'No, no, let him or her come here.'

There were numerous instances when Mandela stopped talking in the middle of addressing a huge rally or some important function taking place in an outdoor stadium, to chastise a security official for treating a child too roughly. These incidents were fairly predictable. A crowd would become unruly usually because the stadium was packed beyond capacity. The result was that the masses surged forward both to get closer to Mandela and to get away from a potential stampede, and small children were usually the first to fall victim to the inherent dangers of this situation. Either they fell down and ran the risk of being trampled, or they would sneak to the front of the crowd and try and climb over a restraining fence. If Mandela noticed this, he would stop speaking and order his bodyguards to rescue a child in danger of being trampled. And woe betide any security official that tried to push a child back over a fence. He would immediately incur the President's wrath and face the humiliation of being shouted at in front of thousands of people. There were occasions at rallies where the President took off his glasses, put his speech down and shouted out publicly to the marshalls or some other security official, 'Go and tell that chap to stop hurting that child. He's hurting the child, stop it now.'

Mandela's own protection unit quickly learnt to respect the President's wishes. They would adopt his attitude in their work, because they had an obligation not only to protect his person but also his integrity and image. They had to preserve who and what he stood for. But it was not as if this had ever been formally conveyed to them. They had not been briefed to behave in this way. *It was a tacit thing, but it was always there and nobody would ever risk defying it.*

Not only would they not defy these unspoken laws, they wouldn't want to. For the 'President of the People' had effectively ensured that his bodyguards became protectors of the people as well. They weren't just acting on instructions; they had internalised the philosophy as well. They all knew that if the President spotted a young child in a crowd, he would invariably stop and instruct his security to bring the child forward. During the state visit of Ghana's President Jerry Rawlins, Mandela spied a young Afrikaner boy watching the pomp and ceremony. *It was ten in the morning, he was in school uniform and I'm not too sure why he wasn't at school. It was a full ceremonial welcome, complete with guards of honour and the playing of the anthems of both countries.*

As Rawlins turned to leave, Mandela stayed behind and beckoned the young boy to come over to the steps of the Union Buildings. Obviously the dumbstruck child didn't move so the President dispatched his Chief of Protocol, John Reinders, to call him. The tiny little figure then had to weave his way through the stern-looking soldiers standing to attention. And in typical fashion Mandela bent down, talked to the little boy, rubbed his head and asked him what his name was, his age, school and what his favourite subjects were. Then he turned to his counterpart and said to the child, 'I'd like you to meet President Jerry Rawlins of Ghana.' The Ghanaian president, to his credit, entered into the spirit of the occasion and had a few words with the boy before being whisked away.

It was so typically Madiba; such a special act of humility. I had tears in my eyes.

AN AFRICAN EXPERIENCE

The way security personnel take on presidential characteristics was probably no more starkly illustrated than on the presidential visits to two African countries – Mali and Togo. Both are Francophone states, and both are in West Africa, but that is where the comparisons end.

The visit to Mali was organised in February 1996. Just getting to the Francophone countries was hard work. There was one direct flight a week from Johannesburg. *To get to Mali, we had to fly from Johannesburg to Paris, wait at Charles de Gaulle Airport for six hours, catch a connecting flight to Brussels and wait for another two hours before finally heading for Mali. Essentially, a 25-hour flight, for a journey that really shouldn't take more than six or seven hours.*

The presidential protection team landed at Mali's capital, Bamako, at about 10 in the evening. For much of the journey they'd enjoyed the comfort of a well air-conditioned cabin. As they stepped out of the plane a wall of humidity assailed them.

As always with ceremonial visits, the official welcome was not scheduled until the next morning, even though the head of state would have been in the country for many hours by then. Mandela arrived a few days after his advance team and was then whisked off to the presidential guesthouse. Mali is a poor country. The guesthouse they provided was very humble. It was essentially a four-bedroom house. There were two bedrooms upstairs where the President and his bodyguard would sleep; the President's secretary and doctor slept downstairs.

Despite having nothing, the people of Mali gave us everything they had. And everything, in this case, meant a massive ticker-tape type parade through the streets of the capital. As was now customary, excited onlookers packed both sides of the roads craning their necks to catch a glimpse of this world-famous leader. The President was driven in an open-top Mercedes Benz and the bodyguards were standing on running boards and holding onto the roof stays of the escort vehicles. One of them was Steyn, who, as the only white person in this massive crowd, was attracting almost as much attention as Mandela.

One Malian soldier was hitting people, literally hitting them with the sling of his rifle and Mandela was shouting, 'No, tell that guy to stop that. He must stop hitting those people.'

But despite this one incident the people of Mali welcomed Mandela with their heart and soul.

From there Mandela went to Togo. The difference was like chalk and cheese.

The chief reason for the visit to Togo was that its president, President Eyadema, had the ear of Nigeria's then military leader Sani Abacha. In 1996 there was an international outcry over the imprisonment and pending execution of Nigerian activist and anti-Abacha campaigner Ken Saro-Wiwa. As the leader who held the moral high ground in Africa, Mandela found himself intervening in the affair. The idea was to encourage Eyadema to speak to Abacha and point out that if he (Abacha) failed to bring his oppressive actions to a halt, he could find himself facing serious international repercussions. (The mission failed because Abacha went ahead with the execution. He was then summarily kicked out of the Commonwealth and found his country facing debilitating punitive sanctions.) Togo's president, unlike that of Mali, was not democratically elected. He was in effect a military dictator, and everyone else behaved like him. The security were pushing and shoving people, behaving like little dictators. Everybody from the President down acted in this dictatorial manner. The differences between the two countries were startling. Both are French-speaking African countries and yet there was this huge gap.

The gap became even more evident as the brief stop in Togo was extended by several hours. The initial idea was just to pop in quickly to Togo *en route* from Mali back to Johannesburg. But Togo's president had other ideas. He was determined to get as much mileage out of this trip as possible. After a quick press conference on landing at the airport, the presidential convoy moved on to Eyadema 's home village. Big American four-by-fours were used as escort vehicles together with two old classic Mercedes Benz cars, one a convertible. The two presidents were standing up in the Mercedes convertible and, in order to gain maximum coverage, an army truck crammed with media representatives travelled in front of the presidential car. The lead security vehicle was then half a kilometre down the road, completely unable to control the situation should a problem arise. But this was all for show.

Once they'd driven a couple of kilometres away from the airport, guards stopped the motorcade, and the presidents were moved to the closed Mercedes. The convoy drove through areas of desperate poverty, eventually ending up at the presidential palace, sickeningly opulent in contrast to what Mandela had just witnessed. Lush gardens bordered on flower-paved expanses. Inside, the floors were of marble, the carpets soft and luxurious. No expense had been spared in a place that screamed ostentation. It was a far cry from Mandela's own humble abode.

On arrival, the rest of the delegation was taken upstairs to a separate room for lunch. The two presidents sat down to lunch while Steyn waited discreetly outside the room, on guard as usual. Eyadema was curious though about the position of this tall white man protecting Mandela. The next minute the Togolese protocol officer called Steyn, saying the president wanted to speak to him. 'Come here, Rory,' echoed Mandela.

The two leaders were seated next to each other at a massive table that could probably seat over 40 people. The only other figure at the table was an interpreter, as Eyadema's English wasn't too good. Before he could say anything, Steyn was beckoned to a seat opposite Mandela, next to the interpreter, and the waiter had arrived to set another place. Steyn had been invited to dine with the two African leaders and during the meal Mandela took the opportunity to explain to Eyadema that this white security official had worked for the former apartheid regime, but was now trusted completely by his new boss.

His lack of airs and graces became one of Mandela's trademarks. And throughout his time in office he was famous for worrying if people around him had eaten or were too hot or cold. He truly regarded everyone as equal and certainly never saw himself as above anybody just because of his station in life.

A MAN FOR ALL PEOPLE

This egalitarian nature was nowhere more clearly demonstrated than when Mandela first moved into his presidential residence in Cape Town. It was at this point, right at the beginning of his term of office, that Mandela was faced with an interesting scenario as the new head of state. And the way he dealt with it set the tone for the rest of his presidential term.

The Cape Town residence of Genadendal is a beautiful place. Set against the backdrop of the majestic Table Mountain, it comprises the very best of South African 'Cape Dutch' architecture and was to become one of Mandela's favourite homes. On his first day in the new setting, he was eager to look around the palatial gardens, and together with his bodyguards he decided to take a little stroll. As he was walking admiringly around the gardens, he noticed that everywhere he went workers were scuttling behind trees, bushes and anything else they could find. This was repeated over and over again. Everywhere he went black workers

– whether they were cleaners, gardeners or other domestic labourers – seemed to vanish the minute he came near them. Now this was certainly a strange situation for Mandela to find himself in. Normally it was the other way round. He would be besieged by people literally falling over each other in their quest to get near him. But in this instance, the more Mandela attempted to get near his staff in a bid to shake their hands, the further away they would run. He was determined to get to the bottom of this. Maybe they were just a little shy or intimidated by their new boss.

All was revealed when the then all-white staff inside the house came and asked him to pose for a group photograph of himself together with all his new employees. Mandela agreed and they quickly gathered together, but without the black workers.

Mandela wasn't having any of this, and said, 'Now call the other workers' (meaning the blacks outside). This request was met with strong resistance. He was told that, 'They couldn't enter as they would make the house dirty.' Mandela just laughed saying, 'That's precisely why there are vacuum cleaners and brooms! They enter here every day precisely so that they can keep the house clean and that's why I want a photo with them.' But when the bodyguards went to call the workers they were met with hostility and a refusal to come up to the main house.

Madiba, not believing that the workers had refused his invitation, went out into the garden and approached the only worker that had not run away again. He extended his hand, which the frightened fellow (a 'coloured' chap) eventually accepted with great hesitancy and a little trepidation. Eventually his colleagues noticed that he was still alive after greeting the President and also came over and accepted Madiba's proffered hand of greeting. After spending some time with them, he managed to penetrate this wall and found out it was not dislike that was keeping them away from their new president but fear. They were scared, they explained, because, 'In the past, under the old South African government, we were told that whenever we see the State President, we must hide.' And failure to do so could even result in dismissal. But all of this changed of course under

Flight

As the gallant silver bird,
Took off, glistening in the
sun,

Taxing where it really can
be heard,
For its early weekly run.

Black smoke streamed
From the engines roaring
But as gay as it seemed
It really was quite boring.

The great silver Boeing
727,
Now, once again in the air
was born,
Rose screaming into
heaven;
Where the other birds were
born.

The pilot, the plane, to port
shall bring,
With all the utmost
caution;
And as it lands, how he
shall sing;
For he knows, he has done
his portion.
           Rory Steyn (12),
     Northcliff Extension 3.

'Flight', a poem I
wrote, published
in *The Star*, 1976.

The Steyn boys from left to right – Rory, Kirby
and Bradly at Dad's house in Northcliff, 1977.

Roosevelt Legends – a great bunch of lads: 5F with Mr Ron Snyman,
November 1981. I am second from left, back row.

Receiving my National Diploma,
August 1987.

Toasting my marriage to Gill, Krugersdorp, 12 December 1987.

'Thorn amongst the roses' – Clifton, Cape Town, with Miss World finalists and chaperones, December 1991.

With the great Gary Player, Bennie Knoetze and FW de Klerk, Nissan Skins, Roodepoort Country Club, October 1991.

One of world music's greats – with Paul Simon in Cape Town during his 'Born at the Right Time' world tour, January 1992.

With Amy Kleinhans at Sun City during the Miss World competition, 1992.

With Miss World 1991 of Venezuela, Ninibeth Leal-Jimenez, Sun City, 1992.

'Out of the sporting wilderness' – at Ellis Park with three All Black legends, Sean Fitzpatrick, Grant Fox and John Kirwan, before the historic isolation-breaking Test, August 1992.

With one of the men I respect most in this world – another All Black, the great Michael Jones, Ellis Park, August 1992.

'White line fever' –
Transvaal rugby
final trials,
February 1993
(with Ian Jones'
All Black socks!).

'When the Aussies
come to dinner' – Ian
Healy, Tim May,
Michael 'Sybil' Slater
and Steve Waugh
(with my son, Kyle),
February 1994. Boy,
did they love bobotie!

Two Victorian gentlemen – with Shane Warne and Merv Hughes, Sun City, March 1994.

Another three All Black greats – with Andrew Mehrtens, Jonah Lomu and Josh Kronfeld, Wanderers Club, June 1995.

Me and my sons, Iain and Kyle, Durban, 1999.

Family photo taken at the boys' nursery school, 1998.

A personal pilgrimage, July 1999, at the monument marking the spot in Howick where Nelson Mandela was arrested in 1962.

Mandela, who instilled in everyone he worked with the maxim that you treat your servants with respect. It was a maxim that filtered down to all of Mandela's bodyguards, that if you treat human beings as human beings, they will respond as such and respect you irrespective of what position you hold.

The fact that Mandela practised this kind of respect was evident at the farewell party he held for his security personnel at the end of his term of office. PPU Head Jason Tshabalala describes it as 'an emotional day, because he was more than just a boss or a president. He was like a father or grandfather to all of us. We used to call him *"Tata"* (grandfather) because that's what he was – we had grown so close to him over the years.' And bearing testament to that closeness was what happened at the end of that party. The bodyguards lined up to have their photographs taken for the last time with this great man. Not only was Mandela happy to do this, but he remembered the names of each and every person who had protected him over the past five years (and we're talking about at least 35 people). In many instances he also had a personal word for them or an enquiry about a sick relative, a new baby or a busy spouse.

DOING THE UNEXPECTED

President Mandela became equally famous for caring not only about his staff but all the citizens of this country. He loved to act in traditionally non-presidential ways – often springing surprises on unsuspecting members of the public as he went about doing the unexpected.

He was well known for paying attention to the smallest of details. This often meant playing the knight in shining armour, which was something Mandela was extremely fond of doing, especially when a young lady was involved. One of the most charming memories is of the day a woman was helped by the most famous of Good Samaritans.

Mandela was being driven to his office by his bodyguards. It was a cold, wet Gauteng morning. And as usual this meant more breakdowns along the freeway than usual. And more breakdowns meant more traffic delays. As the presidential convoy came down Houghton Drive they were faced with a massive traffic jam. There, pulled to one side of the road, was one of its causes: a young lady had a problem with her car. Her vehicle had broken down, resulting in a traffic backlog. Mandela told his driver to stop. This was an unusual request and one that would be frowned upon by those responsible for setting security standards. Presidential convoys did not simply stop in the middle of the road for no obvious reason – it was just too risky and could expose the president to an uncontrolled and potentially dangerous situation. PPU Chief Jason Tshabalala, the Team Leader on the day, quickly popped his head into the President's car to find out what the problem was.

'No problem,' was the reply, 'but clearly this woman whose car is stuck has one.'

'And,' continued Mandela, 'I would like you to assist her in fixing the car!' Tshabalala was momentarily floored, for this constituted a serious breach of security procedures. Presidential convoys were not only instructed not to stop in the middle of the road, but they were specifically instructed not to stop and assist strangers as they could conceivably be part of an ambush. But Mandela refused to listen to these fairly sound and internationally accepted security norms. As far as he was concerned there was a damsel in distress and he was surrounded by able-bodied young men who were more than capable of sorting the problem out! You can imagine the young woman's shock as all these 'men in black' poured out of their fancy vehicles to assist her. By now it was pouring with rain, so they had all donned raincoats and literally held up traffic in a busy intersection while they fixed the woman's car. She was so stunned that she seemed unable to comprehend the fact that these were all the President's men who had been sent to assist her. But no doubt she had a great dinner party story to tell that night and for a long while after!

It wasn't just damsels in distress that caught Mandela's eye. He often went against political correctness, his actions frequently denouncing cheap attempts at popularity. One of these occasions involved the touchy issue of crime. Mandela, like any South African politician, was acutely aware of how bad the crime problem was in the country. It was a subject that evoked strong emotions, particularly from those who had been vicitims of crime and felt that the government wasn't doing enough to contain the problem. By and large, the most vocal of these people were white South Africans, people that Mandela was careful not to alienate as they still held the balance of economic power. And the last thing the President wanted was for them to flee South Africa for the so-called greener pastures abroad. (Although part of his political honesty meant that he frequently spoke his mind and on one occasion said that those who had joined the chicken run were 'traitors'. He later clarified what he had meant by differentiating between those who were offered genuine opportunities abroad and those who ran away complaining about the country's problems.)

At the height of public rage around crime and amid growing calls from some sectors of the community for a return of the death sentence, Mandela went to open a youth detention centre near Newcastle in KwaZulu-Natal. This visit took place in 1996 and the particular centre was the result of a dramatic fund-raising effort.

It was in fact a disused mine that had been turned into a youth centre after a well-known South African mining magnate raised 55 million rand in less than a week to complete that task. It had been renamed 'Ekuseni' and housed juvenile prisoners, many of whom were already hardened criminals jailed for murder and rape. The youths were allowed into a specially erected marquee to listen to the President on the day that he opened Ekuseni. One of them, a 17-year-old youth imprisoned for murder, read a poem that he had composed. It spoke of the folly of what he'd done and how he'd wasted the best years of his life behind bars. Moving stuff. *Ordinarily there would not have been a great deal of sympathy for a ruthless murderer. But this youngster touched a chord with all of us. I know Madiba was particularly moved. He always greeted speakers with a special handshake, but this time he hugged the young man; an action that caused raised eyebrows, but did much to lift the spirit of this kid.*

A SECURITY NIGHTMARE

Of course being a people's president brought with it many wonderful moments, but protecting such a man was hard. While the crowds might have been Mandela's delight and joy, for the bodyguards they were a security nightmare. The President was as famous for his warmth as he was for his spontaneity. And spontaneity in a very popular leader, who could run the risk of assassination, was, as one can imagine, a major headache.

There were so many occasions when Mandela told his bodyguards to just stop the car so that he could get out and meet the people. No sooner had he done this than he was mobbed by thousands of adoring fans and the bodyguards were left to cope with the added pressure that all this involved.

His spontaneity and desire to mingle with the people was to cause many a tough moment for the bodyguards throughout Mandela's five-year term of office. And the stories along this theme are almost too numerous to recall.

First there were the tourists that Mandela would routinely make an effort to greet. This happened on several occasions. For instance one day as he was being driven to his office at the Union Buildings, he noticed a young female tourist enjoying the splendour of the buildings with her little baby. He immediately ordered the convoy to stop and before the bodyguards could protest, he'd hopped out of the car and was greeting the stunned British visitor to South Africa. It was certainly a holiday she'd never forget and probably did more to raise this country in her eyes than any amount of exciting wildlife or visits to beautiful Cape beaches and wine farms. Tourists also became a regular feature at Mandela's Houghton residence in Johannesburg. Busloads of visitors from countries around the world would be taken on a tour of Gauteng, which included the requisite drive past the Houghton presidential residence. The bodyguards had become fairly used to this and were as tolerant of the tour buses as their security code would allow them to be. This meant that the buses could slow down and their occupants could take photographs of the wall around the house. But vehicles were not permitted to stop or let people out. Obviously though, tourists would anxiously scan the entrance to the residence hoping for a glimpse of the world-famous leader. Perhaps they heard stories of the President actually greeting passing tourists.

This was, indeed, not urban legend but very true. And so every busload that went past hoped that today would be their lucky day; that they would pass at just the right time. To be able to go home and say that they had actually met Mandela would provide a lifetime memory. On one occasion Mandela was lunching with apartheid's former Foreign Affairs Minister Pik Botha. He was seeing Botha to his car, when a busload of Brazilian visitors drove past. This was one of those days when Mandela was in a particularly genial mood and keen to mingle with people. The bus caught his attention and he signalled for it to stop and Mandela proceeded to shake each and every person's hand on that bus!

The occupants were delirious with excitement, jabbering away in Portuguese and causing so much chaos that at one point Steyn and his team were forced to manhandle them a little to calm down an increasingly difficult situation. *The little bit of Portuguese we'd learnt in Maputo made no impact!*

But even that, they didn't seem to mind; it was all part of the thrill of actually meeting Mandela. Afterwards Mandela explained to Botha that he liked to go and greet tourists because it meant that they would probably take a good message back home. Botha couldn't agree more, commenting at the time, 'Exactly. It's worth millions, worth millions!'

While that may have been somewhat of an exaggeration, Botha was quite correct in pinpointing the fact that the 'Mandela brand' probably did more for tourism on its own than the game parks and all of South Africa's natural beauty.

But it was not all easy going. *He exasperated us at times, even though most of his actions came out of the goodness of his heart.* On one occasion the bodyguards accompanied Mandela to Lesedi

Clinic in Soweto where his old comrade and prison mate Walter Sisulu had been admitted after falling ill. After the visit, the convoy made its way home past the Baragwanath taxi rank. In the weeks preceeding this occasion, the taxi industry had been wracked by relentless violence which showed no signs of abating as rival taxi groups fought a bitter turf war. For precisely this reason and on the spur of the moment, Mandela decided that this was an excellent opportunity to get out of the vehicle and speak to local taxi drivers and find out about some of their grievances first hand. His bodyguards, of course, thought the complete opposite. There had been no advance planning and anything could happen in an unprotected and insecure environment such as this one, particularly an environment that had seen terrible bloodshed only a few days ago. *I tried to talk him out of it, but I knew I was wasting my time. Instead I knew I had to start thinking of alternative ways to deal with this sticky situation. I managed to convince Madiba to remain in the car until we had gained control on the ground. He agreed to do this and eventually got out and addressed the taxi drivers. That was typical Mandela, President of the People, and we just had to adapt. We quickly learnt that instead of trying to change him, we had to find creative ways of dealing with his wishes and impulses and tailoring our strategies accordingly.*

COURTING DANGER

Just as Mandela's desire for reconciliation put him in the line of fire, so too being a people's president meant that Mandela probably courted danger far more often than most leaders. There was a genuine love of people about the man. A colleague once commented, 'If you could bottle Mandela's charm and charisma and sell it around the world, somebody would be very rich and leaders around the globe would be flocking to buy it.'

For many heads of state what's known as 'pressing flesh' is all part of the job. Those casual handshakes, kissing of babies, hugging the elderly and diligently doing one's bit for children and the environment are the kind of things that take up a leader's time, but are rarely things they would genuinely choose to do.

And even worse, most people regard these actions somewhat cynically, aware that they are for show and usually on the increase around election time, as would-be heads of state go about their vote-grabbing exercises.

Mandela was one of those rare exceptions. He seemed to thrive whenever he was called upon to mingle with the people. Addressing rallies or touring local communities was his favourite pastime and one he accomplished with ease and a genuine sense of enjoyment.

At rallies he would always take time to personally thank the organisers, entertainers, police officers and others involved. *He would never leave any venue without personally greeting the choir and the police.* This was another security headache, as bodyguards had to oversee long queues of people lining up to shake Mandela's hand and perhaps receive a personal word from him. Added to this was the fact that he was taking the very people needed to maintain some semblance of public order (the police) away from their posts to thank them!

And it was precisely in these kinds of situations that the element of personal danger was heightened – uncontrolled or 'non-sterile' environments in security slang. Anything could happen and the bodyguards had to be even more alert than usual. For them the biggest danger was not a sinister assassin lurking behind every corner, but the ecstatic love of the people Mandela was meeting. Tshabalala says, 'It's not that people always want to harm the President, but out of love for him they start pushing forward and causing chaos. Mandela used to remark that "People can kill you out of love". ' And it was this almost oppressive love that the bodyguards had to learn to accommodate in working for Mandela.

Madiba liked to tell the story of his visit to the late Professor Johan Heyns's Dutch Reformed Church (the largest Afrikaner denomination) in Pretoria, before Heyns was murdered by an assassin's bullet. As he was leaving after his address, he was mobbed by Afrikaner church-goers wanting to shake his hand. The crush and confusion was so bad that Madiba lost his shoe! He would always remark that, 'a few years ago these people wanted to kill me out of hate. Now they nearly killed me out of love!'

Gradually, however, the bodyguards became used to this and would often pre-empt the President in organising children to come forward and meet him at rallies and special events. But Mandela's lack of personal regard often went too far – at least as far as the bodyguards were concerned. Mandela's first thought was always for the people around him, while his bodyguards' first concern was obviously for their leader. This led to several clashes. On one occasion, at the height of the ANC–IFP violence in 1994, Mandela was attending a township rally in Umlazi where he was the keynote speaker. A volley of gunshots rocked the stadium. People began to panic and his protectors advised him to leave the place immediately. Mandela refused point-blank, saying that a true leader did not flee a scene at the first sign of trouble. Instead he insisted on staying in the stadium until everyone else had been evacuated. When the President's mind was made up he would not budge. Refusing to don a bulletproof vest, he insisted on completing his speech and there was just no point in arguing with him. Instead the bodyguards threw a protective cordon around him, brought the cars closer and hoped for the best. *This shouldn't have happened and wouldn't have later on in his presidency. I think that at the time, so soon after his release, the guys were more than a little in awe of Nelson Mandela. He should have been taken away from there immediately whether he liked it or not!*

It was not, however, the first time that this happened. The bodyguards got a taste of things to come when, prior to Mandela's election as president, a similar scenario developed. It was at the Jabulani amphitheatre in Soweto, just after the assassination of Communist Party leader Chris Hani in April 1993. The situation was tense and volatile, emotions were running high and South Africa could literally have spun out of control at any minute. Shots were fired, the presidential cars were bashed about and the bodyguards insisted that they should leave. Again,

Mandela would not hear of it and refused to budge until everyone had been evacuated safely.

These events were to have an ugly sequel many years later during Mandela's term of office. *Undoubtedly my worst day as a protection officer was when Madiba decided, at the suggestion of Jacob Zuma (now Deputy President), to attend the funerals of ANC members killed in violence in the Natal Midlands, specifically the violence-wracked area of Richmond.* Natal Midlands warlord and subsequently assassinated IFP leader Sifiso Nkabinde was widely believed to have been behind the killings. The ANC felt it was important that Mandela show support for his followers by attending the funerals. *I got a phone call on the Friday night to say that Madiba would attend the funerals on the Sunday, giving me only Saturday – one day – to get down to KwaZulu-Natal and do the advance planning.* Steyn was joined by the regional planning officer Deon Botha, and on his arrival the pair met up with Dr Zweli Mkhize, Provincial Health Minister and prominent ANC leader. It was decided that Mandela would fly to the strife-torn region by helicopter as this would minimise any potential dangers. He would attend the funeral briefly and then leave as quickly as possible. *We had very little time available to do proper planning and all agreed that this would be the best course of action. All our routes were planned and everyone was properly briefed. Madiba, however, as usual had other ideas. Upon his arrival he informed us that he wanted to fly into the area controlled by Nkabinde, land the chopper and walk around there. He would then go to the funeral in his convoy. We all protested, but knew that our cries were in vain. Madiba was determined to walk through Nkabinde's turf. It was his way of telling Nkabinde that he didn't 'control' any area of the country.*

Steyn sprang into emergency action, telephoning Botha and the advance team to arrange for a police Nyala (armoured personnel carrier) with smoke grenades and to go and identify a landing zone. The result was that the presidential party landed in the middle of nowhere and Mandela was insistent that he go to a place that was densely populated with Nkabinde's supporters. *Again, he was not sticking to the script! He wanted Nkabinde's people to see him walking around there.* The problem was that the only vehicle there was the police Nyala but Mandela refused to drive in this, as it could be interpreted in the wrong way politically, namely that the police sided with the ANC. This, of course, would have made their already difficult job even more problematic. *In the end we were forced to wait for the local police to arrive and use an ordinary unarmoured vehicle that would not be identified as a police car, as the President's armoured car was waiting at the original spot as per our briefing. The upshot of this was that we drove directly past Nkabinde's house in an unprotected vehicle. We could actually see the warlord's men gathering, one of them carrying an assault rifle. At this point Madiba wanted to get out and stop at a shop. But here I drew the line and flatly refused.* The convoy drove a little further and eventually stopped about 1 km down the road where Mandela got out and greeted people at a kraal there. This of course caused a massive traffic jam making the bodyguards' job even more complicated. *I still go cold when I think of that day. I was praying almost non-stop. We had taken a massive chance driving past Nkabinde's house in a 'soft vehicle', but that's all part and parcel of protecting a people's president. It's certainly not only all crayfish and caviar.*

A SPECIAL COMMITMENT TO CHILDREN

While Mandela was certainly a president for all people, a man with the common touch, equally at home with kings and queens as he was with the poorest of the poor, it was children that had always captured his heart.

It has been well documented here and elsewhere that the President has a special regard for children. He could never turn them away and they would always be the first to be singled out in a crowd for a privileged word with the President. And over the years, Mandela learnt to charm even the most shy of children. *His approach was a well-honed one. He would always ask, 'What's your name?' followed up with, 'And who gave you that lovely name?' He then wanted to know how old they were, what standard at school they were in and their favourite subject. If the answer was science or maths that would get an extra round of approval, 'Oh, very good!' with Madiba commenting how much the country needed scientists and engineers. Then he would ask what they wanted to be when they grew up and if the answer was a doctor, Madiba would smile conspiratorially and joke, 'Oh, I won't get sick then until you can personally treat me!' And if on the rare occasion a child was too scared to greet Madiba, he would tease them saying, 'One day, I'll be as important as you are and then I won't greet you either!'*

Probably the definitive story on Madiba and children is the one regarding the establishment of the Nelson Mandela Children's Fund.

Mandela tells the story about how he came out of a building somewhere in Cape Town at around five or six in the evening to find a group of 12 to 15 street children waiting for him. 'My security, who are very vigilant, stopped these children running to me and I asked them, "Why do you stop them?"

"Because they are dirty and look how they are dressed."

"Precisely for that reason, let them come to me."

"These children came to me and asked me, why do you love us?"

"How do you know that I love you?"

"Because you gave us money"

'They were referring to the money I had received from the Nobel foundation when I was awarded the Nobel Peace Prize, which I had given to various children's charities. I told these children that I had not worked for this money and that is why I'd given it to charity. That night I could not sleep. All I could think about were these children and what they had said to me. This was when I decided to give one third of my salary towards a fund to deal specifically with children.' And it was called the Nelson Mandela Children's Fund.

Another typical Madiba characteristic was his penchant for 'teaching' children to sing *Twinkle, Twinkle, Little Star*. Whenever he visited a school (which is something he did quite often) the children would have something specially prepared to sing for him. He would patiently listen to them with his hands clasped together in front of him and a smile on his face. Thereafter he would ask them if he could teach them a song.

'Would you like that?' he would ask before launching into a pretty good tenor rendition of the well-known kiddies' song. It seemed that things had changed since Madiba went to school, because no one seemed to know the tune he sang! However, as soon as he finished his solo he always asked the children to join him the second time round and they had no problem adapting to his tune!

He did this for his grandson, Mbuso, when he surprised him by paying a visit to his school to wish him 'happy birthday'.

A simple act like surprising your grandson at school on his birthday is never quite simple if the grandfather happens to be Nelson Mandela! The entire day's education came to a standstill as utter pandemonium broke out throughout the school. Children were running to him from all directions as soon as the word got out (which took about 7 ½ seconds). It was clear that Madiba's love of children was wholly mutual!

There were three annual practices that were simply a part of the President's life. One was that he would visit about eight to ten crèches in Johannesburg and Cape Town every year. Madiba would arrive with lots of sweets, chips and so on, kindly sponsored by various sweet and chocolate makers and dish them out to the children. He would issue careful instructions that the crèches should be those attended by underprivileged children of all races.

The rewards were great, as these children were so very appreciative. It said a lot about their needs that they were more interested in sweets than meeting President Mandela.

Another occasion was the children's party held in honour of his birthday. In July every year, during school holidays, Madiba would host a massive, national children's party. It was an enormous logistical exercise with children bussed into a central venue from all over the country. One year, for example, he concentrated solely on so-called 'street children' and another year on handicapped children.

Children's TV show hosts and well-known animal characters were all there and instead of attending to the rigours of office and global political problems, he would spend the day brightening up the lives of a few thousand children.

The final event was the Christmas party for all the children of his hometown of Qunu and the surrounding areas. While not quite on the same scale, it also involved huge logistical planning and sponsors' support and Zelda la Grange would be at it basically as soon as the birthday party was over. Sheep were slaughtered and a fine feast laid on at the President's farm.

This event brought particular happiness to the children in the rural areas of Umtata. Being an unexposed, unadvertised event, some children walked barefoot for two days to attend the only event of the year when they would receive sweets and presents. Approximately 4 500 children attended the party on Christmas Day 1998.

I saw an incredible photograph of the President and a blind boy 'seeing' Madiba. He had his hands on the President's face, an emotional expression of concentration on his face, while Madiba's face was one of curious delight as he concentrated on keeping still for this child. That just summed up the essence of this unbelievable, unique relationship that he had with children. Even those who had never met him knew him instantly from media images and rushed up to him quite unabashedly should they ever see him in the flesh. As a father, it is something that has never ceased to absolutely amaze me.

$$\text{``} \bullet \bullet \bullet$$

A true story as told by
Nelson Mandela

I was sitting in my lounge one day when security came in and told me that there was a young lady to see me at the gate. They said, 'Mr President we must warn you, she is very arrogant.' Precisely for that reason I let her come in. She came into the lounge; she was about five years old. She did not greet me. She merely asked, 'How old are you?' I replied, 'Well, I don't know. I can't remember, but I was born a long, long time ago.'

'How long ago – two years, five years?'

'I said I told you I can't remember, but it was long ago.'

'Well then, who sent you to jail?'

'Well I didn't go there because I wanted to. Some people sent me there.'

'How long were you there?'

'I can't remember, but it was a long time.'

'How long – two years, five years?'

'No, I can't remember, but it was a long time.' Realising these questions were futile, she looked at me and said, 'You, you are a stupid old man!'

$$\bullet \bullet \bullet \text{''}$$

3

The World Comes to South Africa

' By the way, who are these Spice Girls?'
(A question asked by Mandela prior to
meeting the British all-girl band.)

Not only did Nelson Mandela travel the world during his presidency, but the world came to South Africa to meet him. And it wasn't only the requisite heads of state and government that did so. Pop stars, Hollywood actors and actresses, sporting legends, princes, princesses, kings and queens trooped off to Africa's southern-most tip, often primarily in the hope that they would receive a much-coveted audience with Madiba.

Once the ANC was unbanned, sanctions against South Africa were slowly lifted. This opened the door to the rest of the world; and for the first time this country was exposed to the culture, sports and technology it had been denied because of its apartheid policies. Places like Cape Town became a hot destination for the rich and famous. But there was one person whose attraction out-stripped all of South Africa's natural beauty and world-famous game. When it came to desirability, Mandela was without doubt South Africa's number one drawcard. Tourists would drive past his house eager for a glimpse. And while the lifting of sanctions meant sports teams and pop stars could now add South Africa to their agenda, it was often the Mandela-brand that would finally clinch a deal. Many a musician has agreed to perform in South

Africa on the understanding that a trip to this country could also include a prized few minutes with a living legend.

PAUL SIMON

Even before Mandela became President, South Africa was becoming a favoured destination among politicians and pop stars alike. And even prior to his appointment to Mandela's team, Steyn was to have the privilege of working with leading figures from the political, sports and cultural arenas.

Teenagers living in the post-Mandela era have become blasé about visiting pop stars. Today, South Africa is besieged by a plethora of world-famous bands, and like the rest of the world has the very best to choose from on a regular basis. But shortly after sanctions were lifted, visiting pop stars (that weren't has-beens lured to Sun City by the promise of lots of money) were a novelty. And so when the first really big name came to this country, there was massive interest from both the public and the media. That honour was to fall to Paul Simon, who came to South Africa in 1992 to round off his 'Born At the Right Time' world tour. He'd been on the road for 13 months and the South African concerts were numbers 163–168 (including one in Gaborone). This really was the first big musical event in South Africa since the lifting of the cultural boycott.

But although the lifting of the boycott obviously had the approval of the ANC, not all political parties supported this. More militant black organisations like the Azanian People's Orgnanisation (Azapo) were vehemently opposed to Simon's presence. It's hard to imagine now, but the concert took place under massive security. A ring of steel was thrown around Ellis Park Stadium, where the first of his concerts would take place; and police in cars, on foot and on horseback patrolled the area. The youth wing of Azapo had set the tone when they threw a hand grenade into the offices of concert promoters Pro-sound (later to become Big Concerts). This occurred one morning at about 2:00 a.m. Promoter Attie van Wyk was called out to the scene. Also on stand-by that night was Lieutenant Rory Steyn, who was dispatched to the scene as the explosives expert. After an arduous on-site investigation, Steyn finally headed for home, absolutely exhausted. He'd just got into bed, when he got another call from Van Wyk. 'Rory, please come down to the Carlton Hotel now, they want to cancel the tour,' was his frantic message. *So I got back into my clothes, back into my car and drove to the Carlton. There was a small gathering in Paul Simon's executive suite. Simon was there, looking rather alarmed but still keen to continue with the tour.* Simon asked Steyn what he thought. His immediate response was that Azapo represented a very small minority. *They were the loony left, I told him. The majority of South Africans wanted the tour to go ahead. He seemed reassured by my response and requested that I be assigned to him for the rest of the tour. It was a wonderful experience for me, because there was no one in South Africa at that stage with any knowledge of concert security, simply because we had never had any real international acts out here yet.* Steyn made sure that he learnt everything he could from Simon's security officials – lessons that were to stand him in good stead many years later. *The head of the Crime Intelligence Service authorised me to tour nationwide with Paul Simon, who was very generous, paying me a daily rate for my services. It was my first experience of moonlighting. My work was cut out for me, as there were demonstrations at each concert. But they were small and certainly not vocal enough to stop the concerts going ahead. And as the tour progressed and received such a fantastic response, the protests started losing momentum as it was plain to see that they really did have the support of a very small minority grouping.* Steyn found Simon a very intelligent, down-to-earth person, extremely approachable with none of the airs and graces that many a famous person often puts on. And Simon was also very interested in Steyn's views on South Africa's future. *I remember the day that they were due to leave South Africa. We were having breakfast together and Paul Simon asked me, 'Rory, how do you see South Africa turning out?' (This was still during the CODESA period and South Africa's future hung under a cloud of uncertainty.) I answered that I was optimistic, that I thought it would one day be a great country. Although I*

*was still something of a racist in those days, but generally believed
that things could get better in South Africa. One of the few regrets I
have is that I never went on any of Mandela's American trips because
I would have loved to have rung up Paul Simon (for he had invited me
to do so) and continue that conversation. I think he would have
enjoyed learning that I'd become Nelson Mandela's protection team
leader.*

THE END OF STEVE WAUGH?

In addition to hosting international pop stars, it was also Steyn's
privilege to work with some of the world's leading sporting figures. Being a huge sports fan, this was one area of his job that he
absolutely loved and which always felt more like fun than hard
work. Just as the cultural boycott had been lifted, so was the sports
boycott. This meant that before long, South Africa was now hon-
ourably (as opposed to sneaking in rebel tours) pitting its sports-
men and women against the very best the world had to offer. In
1994 the Australian cricket tour of South Africa took place and
Steyn was given the responsibility for the team's safety for the
Gauteng leg of the tour. This was normal procedure, but assumed
an added risk on this particular visit for a number of reasons.

South Africa had just finished touring Australia at the end of
1993 and the series was shared. South African fans had
watched on television how the Australian fans had abused
South Africans and they were just itching to pay back. The tour
also took place against the backdrop of an extremely volatile
South Africa. It ended just days before South Africa's historic
1994 all-race elections and so the visiting team experienced all
the fear, paranoia and excitement in the build-up to that historic
day. Man of the Series in both the One Day Internationals
(ODIs) and Tests, Steve Waugh, wrote in his Tour Diary on
April 5:

> Our fears as we travelled through the townships were yet
> another reminder of the fragile state of the country. It has
> been impossible not to notice the increasing media reports
> of violence of late, even if we have not come into direct

contact with any disturbances. But as the April 27 election draws closer the potential for a bloody confrontation grows by the day. As recently as the final day of the third Test, a massacre occurred after a Zulu march was met by supporters of the ANC. At least 15 people died in the battle. Most of the team have the feeling that something dreadful will happen shortly, and, to be honest, we cannot wait to get out of the country before such carnage erupts.

Waugh was of course referring here to the so-called Shell House Massacre in which the ANC and the IFP had a bloody confrontation resulting in horrific bloodshed and an escalation of tension ahead of the elections.

The pressure of this backlash from the fans and perhaps the political tensions caused Shane Warne and Merv Hughes to lose their heads during the first Test at the Wanderers and incur both huge fines and the ire of South Africans.

The Aussies left for Sun City straight after losing that Test. The next day, 9 March, was spent viewing game, relaxing in The Valley of Waves and playing golf. Steyn of course accompanied them. It was while enjoying the innocent fun of playing around on the many water rides that it happened. The setting was one of the water tube rides called The Viper which twists and turns in total darkness. *As you are lying on your back, moving at quite a rate, you have absolutely no idea which way or when the next twist in the tube will be and it culminates in a splashdown into a pool at the bottom of the ride. This is the first time you see daylight since entering the tube.*

Steve Waugh went just before me. I waited for much longer than the safety steward indicated I should, before I followed him into The Viper's mouth. Towards the end of the ride, I was really moving. Keeping my swimming costume out of the water (as it causes too much drag) I was making contact with the tube only with my heels and shoulder blades. Next moment I slammed into something human with a sickening jolt, eliciting an anguished scream, before both Steve and I tumbled out into the pool.

It was an awful moment for Steyn, who knew only too well that he might have caused a serious injury. Not only had they collided very hard, but Steyn was quite a bit bigger than Waugh. *When I saw his face, I was really worried. My right heel had slammed into the small of Steve's back, into that muscle next to the spine, as he was sitting upright in the tube, trying to push himself forward. I raced off to find the Aussie physio "Hooter", as I knew from rugby experience to start treatment before the muscle cools down.*

Well, that certainly put an end to the relaxation and enjoyment for Steve Waugh as he was on the physio's bench at least twice a day every day for the rest of the tour. Writing in his Tour Diary more than a week later on the first day of the second Test in Cape Town, he reports: 'My lower back and buttocks are still extremely stiff and sore from my Sun City incident.'

It is a tribute to this player's mental strength and true Aussie grit that he helped them to victory by scoring 86 in the first innings and taking his best ever Test haul of 5 for 28 in our second, deservedly earning him yet another Man of the Match. My sorrow at our loss and that of the series lead was tempered by the knowledge that I hadn't done as serious damage to Aussie's brightest star as I originally thought I had. However the Tour Diary reflects a week later, on 24 March, 'The back problem that resulted from the kick in the back at the Sun City waterslide refuses to go away.'

Three years later, in 1997, the Australians returned to South Africa. By this time Steyn was well established in his job as Mandela's Team Leader. However he made time to catch up with the Australian team. *When I saw Steve Waugh the first thing I asked was, 'How's the back, Tugga?'*

'Still sore, mate!' was the reply. He went on to explain that it never really goes away and it is one of those aches and pains he'll always have to live with.

It is a measure of his character that Steve has never held that accident against me. A lesser person might have allowed it to affect a relationship. I admire that. But sometimes I still get a chill when I think of how close I came to doing some serious damage, possibly paralysing this great cricketer. He was ranked the number one batsman in the world at the time and without a doubt was the crucial difference between two evenly matched sides in 1994.

ENGLAND PHYSIO ARRESTED FOR ILLEGAL SUBSTANCES

Next it was the turn of the English Cricket team. And once again the man on the security beat was Rory Steyn. The first Test of the 95/96 England Tour of South Africa, at Centurion Park, was severely affected by rain. Steyn was in the English dressing room during one such rain delay when he asked their physio, Wayne Morton, to have a look at his hamstring as he was suffering from a rugby injury. *He had me hop up onto his bench, checked and treated me, then informed me that he was going to give both legs a rub. I thought nothing of it, there was nothing going on cricket-wise so I started reading a magazine lying, obviously, on my tummy. Next moment I've got the whole Pommie touring team singing 'happy birthday' to me and laughing their heads off! Morton had found out that it was my birthday. He'd spread cricket-boot whitener all over the back of both legs and got the boys around to see his handiwork at my expense!*

Robyn Smith, the Durban-born middle-order batsman who chose to play for England during the isolation years, in part put out that his South African mate had been 'had'; but probably also due to his own mischievous nature, quietly suggested to Steyn that this lark could not go unpunished. *I began to devise a plan.*

England went to Bloemfontein for a three-day game against Free State before returning to Johannesburg for the Wanderers Test. Steyn had rung up the England manager, John Barclay, and let him in on his intentions. He was due to meet the team at the airport and so decided to get down there an hour or so earlier. Once there he looked up a few colleagues at the airport's Drug Squad. *I explained my plan and they were keen to help.*

And what a plan it was. *Picture this: As the team arrived and was waiting for their luggage, two uniformed police officers and a Drug Squad detective approached the team and asked for 'Mr Morton, the physiotherapist'. I was well out of sight, observing this spectacle from an upper balcony. The policemen approached Wayne and asked him to collect all his luggage and follow them. His immediate response was, 'Did Rory Steyn put you up to this?'*

To their credit, my colleagues remained poker-faced. John Barclay reacted with all the necessary indignation and told Wayne in his clipped Cambridge accent to accompany the police, but not to worry as he was speaking to their solicitor!

The police then took Wayne down to the Drug Squad offices and informed him that they suspected him of importing illegal substances into South Africa. They demanded a complete list of all the medication he'd brought with him. This was designed to give enough time to the rest of the team to board the bus and head off for the hotel. *I joined the team on the bus and they whole-heartedly approved of this devious scheme. Once we had left the airport I called my colleagues and gave the all-clear for them to bring Wayne to the hotel.*

The Sandton Sun had a traditional welcome of cocktails in the lobby whenever the team returned. I got all the players to wait there and we weren't disappointed. Morton arrived in the back of a yellow South African Police van. It dropped him at the front door to the hotel and the first thing he saw as the van door swung open was the flash of a tabloid photographer's camera (briefed by us) in the full glare of an astounded public and hotel staff!

The next thing he saw was the rest of the team laughing their heads off with Steyn behind them. Only then did he realise that it was, in fact, all a huge prank.

He greeted me with a hug and more than a little relief and a Yorkshire-accented, 'You bastard!'

The incident made it into The Independent *as a tongue-in-cheek article and cemented a great friendship between Wayne and me that endures to this day.*

THE ALL BLACKS AND FOOD POISONING
It wasn't all cricket either. Steyn also had the privilege of working on the historic 1995 Rugby World Cup. The Cabinet took a decision that each of the 16 participating teams would receive two permanent protectors that would travel with them. Steyn

was assigned the All Blacks, having worked with them in 1992. They arrived and started the tournament quietly with defending champions Australia and hosts South Africa receiving all the attention. But as the tournament progressed it was the All Blacks and their phenomenal winger, Jonah Lomu, that began to grab the headlines.

The Springboks grimly held on in the rain against France in the first semi-final and Lomu single-handedly demolished England in the other, to set up the Dream Final: SA vs NZ. *Up until then things had been easy going in the All Black camp. Their coach, Laurie Mains, had kindly allowed me to train with the All Blacks and there is no doubt that they were the best team of the tournament, playing the best rugby.*

However, as soon as the finalists were determined, the entire South African contingent on tour with the All Blacks was ostracised. Instead of going to the Sandton Sun, which is where the finalists were scheduled to stay, the New Zealand management asked to return to the Crowne Plaza, which is where they had stayed for the majority of the tournament. *This was against our advice, but they weren't listening to us.* All Blacks captain Sean Fitzpatrick is quoted in his biography, *'Turning Point',* as saying:

'In hindsight we probably should have gone away, found another hotel out of the hype of Johannesburg. We were well looked after. The South African organisation was as good as any and they went out of their way to make sure it was the best. It really was superb – until that last week when everything changed. The first night a car alarm went off all night, every two hours. We asked why it wasn't stopped and the reply was that they were having trouble with the tow-trucks and that moving the car was a security risk because of the fear of bombs. And phone calls were suddenly coming through. People were ringing saying, 'Fitzpatrick, you're going to lose on Saturday.' When you asked how that could suddenly happen, the excuse was, 'Sorry, we had a new guy on last night who didn't know the procedure'.

At the last team meeting the South Africans were permitted to attend, a tense Mains said, 'It happened to "Tree" (Colin Meads) in 1970, it happened to me in 1976. I want a man assigned 24 hours to Jonah; he doesn't move anywhere without a bodyguard!' I think that Mains was referring to dubious occurrences on those two All Black tours, as they had taken place at the height of the Afrikaner Broederbond's quest to control South African rugby, as a symbol of Afrikaner strength and domination. Fortunately, then South African Rugby Board president, Dr Danie Craven, stubbornly resisted this 'hijacking' of South African rugby.

Fitzpatrick admits that Mains was paranoid, perhaps justifiably so. But it was rubbing off on his players who had to wait to have the team room 'swept' for electronic bugs before each team session, in case the South Africans were recording the All Blacks' talks and tactics.

Mains had ordered a separate dining room too, to get the team out of the public glare.

The separate dining room was a major mistake. If we had had any say, I would have strongly advised against it. The All Blacks had been eating their meals in a cordoned-off area in the main hotel dining room up until then. Anyone wanting to poison the team would therefore have had to poison every other guest as well and the hotel was packed to capacity.

On the Thursday night before the final, Steyn took a bunch of players to a movie at Sandton City. This was one way of relieving the tension, although by then, the guys had seen most of the movies. The result was that everyone was scattered throughout the various cinemas. Steyn watched a movie with Richard Loe and when it finished he noticed that he looked wretched. Jeff Wilson was watching another much longer movie and ordinarily the guys would have waited for him by playing arcade games. *Loey, however, wanted to go straight back, so I said I would go and tell Goldie (Wilson) that I would come back for him. As I approached the doors to his cinema, he came out clutching his stomach, almost doubled over. I immediately knew we had a serious problem. We raced back to the hotel. Loey didn't even make it to the flowerbed. He vomited all over the driveway. When I got upstairs to the doctor's room it looked like a battle zone; like a scene from a war movie – players were lying all over the place and the doctor and physio were walking around injecting them. Now, I was a police officer, I worked with facts. What my eyes told me that night was that the team had deliberately been poisoned.*

It is fair to say that because this happened on the Thursday, and the medical staff had got it under control on the Friday, that the players were physically okay (with the exception of Wilson and possibly Mehrtens) by Saturday afternoon. But what of their mental side? Compare their build-up to that of the Springboks. *It was one of the toughest few days of my life. I had to endure accusations of complicity in this by a New Zealand official and I was very angry that this was allowed to happen in my country to people 'in my care'.*

When the All Blacks took to the field on that historic day, 24 June 1995, I wanted them to win. THAT, is hard for me to say. It was only when I heard that huge crowd of mainly white South Africans start to chant their President's name, 'Nelson, Nelson, Nelson' that my patriotism returned.

What a hugely brave show the All Blacks put on that day. Wilson could never have lasted and so was replaced by Marc Ellis. They were the better side but we were better on the day. Against unbelievable South African patriotic fervour (anyone who was there will never forget the electric atmosphere), against the effects of Ellis Park's 5 400 ft altitude and against food poisoning, they ran South Africa close (into extra time), so close!

Laurie Mains, now the highly popular coach of the Golden Lions, says that he will go to his grave wondering what would have happened if the All Blacks had not been sick. Mains employed a private investigator in an attempt to get to the bottom of it. The investigator's report to Mains was that a Far-Eastern betting syndicate had paid a waitress called Suzie at the All Blacks' hotel to put something into the All Blacks' water. South African rugby fans remain sceptical of this theory and prefer to put it down to 'sour Kiwi grapes'.

To my fellow South Africans I want to say this: stop all those cheap jokes about 'Suzie', the 'food poisoning' and 'whingeing Kiwis'.

It happened. There is no doubt that the All Blacks were poisoned two days before the Final. The All Black team never whinged about it. If anyone whinged it was their media (and boy, can they whinge!).

In fact the New Zealand team management took a decision not to use the poisoning as an excuse, not to even mention it. It was only when the New Zealand media got wind of it and directly asked the team management at media conferences, 'What about the food poisoning in the hotel before the Final?', that they spoke about it. We must learn to be gracious winners, we must shed our boorish image. Our victory over such a magnificent side makes it that much more of an achievement. And the '95 All Blacks were that – a magnificent side.

MANDELA – SOUTH AFRICA'S NUMBER ONE DRAWCARD

If Steyn thought he had it good in the years just prior to Mandela's presidency, it was nothing compared to the many people he was privileged to encounter during the years he worked for the President.

During his five years as head of state, there was nobody that Mandela could not have an audience with. It's amazing that a man who was just short of 80, and who had spent nearly a third of his life in prison, convicted of sabotage, was one of the most sought-after people in the world. Everyone's hero, Mandela was instantly recognisable. Every famous person that entered this country would do so in the hope that they would meet the President. And most of them managed to do just that. Hollywood stars, musicians and super models all fell for the Madiba Magic. And while at first it was a novelty to see some super-celebrity hugging the President, after a while it became almost boring.

Mandela met many celebrities, but he had absolutely no idea why some of them were famous. However there were a few he particularly enjoyed.

Certainly his meeting with Princess Diana – about a year before her death – ranked high with him. And his attendance at the 'Bravo! Africa' Three Tenors concert at the Union Buildings in 1999 was one of his favourite occasions – so much so that he stayed after half-time, something Mandela rarely does.

There is also the famous story of Mandela meeting actor Eddie Murphy for the first time. The star was queueing with a host of other Hollywood names to shake Mandela's hand at a banquet in New York. Imagine his surprise when Mandela turned to him and said, 'Oh hello Eddie, how are you?' Murphy was shocked that Mandela even knew who he was let alone would greet him by his first name. It turns out that *Beverly Hills Cop*, starring Murphy, was one of the few movies Mandela and his fellow cell mates had actually managed to see inside prison. There were other stars, notably those who had contributed to the anti-apartheid struggle, whom Mandela always had a lot of time for. Singers like Stevie Wonder, Nina Simone, Harry Belafonte and Diana Ross and actors like Danny Glover were firm favourites with the President, meeting him on more than one occasion and having a special place at his 80th birthday party. And superstar Michael Jackson really hit it big with Mandela. He was invited to several of Mandela's birthday parties. But even in such an intimate context, the superstar was unable to relax. He would greet Mandela and then retire to a corner, not speaking to anyone else for the rest of the evening.

Sporting figures – legends in their own right – paled in comparison to Mandela.

Soccer great Pelé gave Mandela his number 10 jersey and boxing legend Mohammed Ali gave Mandela a signed pair of gloves.

And then there were beauty queens aplenty. On the three occasions that the Miss World contests were held in South Africa, Mandela met every one of the 80-odd beauty queens. And astonishingly, he knew the names of the leaders of every single one of those 80-odd countries, and in most cases had a personal word for that particular head of state as well.

Another story that springs to mind is the whole Naomi Campbell 'honorary granddaughter' thing. She has totally misconstrued what Madiba meant. He must have at some stage referred to her as his 'granddaughter' and this went straight to her head. What she doesn't realise is that Mandela calls all of his staff, his security and anyone of that age, his grandchildren. It's part of African culture and the way we refer to each other. She has made far too much of it and simply illustrates what is meant by black Americans (in her case black Brits) missing the point by saying that coming to South Africa is coming back to their roots, when they don't have the slightest knowledge of African culture. Many whites in South Africa have remarked on numerous occasions that they are far more African than these foreigners.

I consider myself to be an African. The closest I come to my European heritage is three generations away. I am therefore totally African. My parents were born in Africa and so were my grandparents, and these people cannot consider themselves to be anything other than American or British.

"...

A true story as told by
Nelson Mandela

I was on holiday recently in the Bahamas and was taking a walk one day. I passed a man and his wife – also out walking. The man stopped me and asked, 'Aren't you Nelson Mandela?' I replied that many people mistake me for that chap. He looked at his wife and said, 'Darling, this is Mr Nelson Mandela.' She was totally unimpressed. He repeated it, this time more firmly, 'Darling, this is Nelson Mandela.' She remained unimpressed and asked, 'Well, what is he famous for?'

..."

4

An International Icon

If they don't like it, they can go and jump in a pool.
(Mandela responding to US criticism
of his friendship with Libya.)

Nelson Mandela may have spent 27 years in jail, but he certainly made up for lost time in the period following his release. During the five years of his presidency Mandela travelled the world, visiting over 70 countries and hosting the equivalent number of leaders. In fact, he was so much in demand that he was forced to turn down dozens of invitations.

What follows is snapshots of a small number of his many visits abroad.

UNITED KINGDOM

One of the most high-profile and successful international trips was Mandela's state visit to the United Kingdom in July of 1996.

The super-efficient British Metropolitan Police had two protection units. Obviously, from its name, the Royalty Protection Unit ensured the safety of the entire royal family, while the Special Branch co-ordinated the Prime Minister's security and all other VIP protection, including visiting heads of state and government.

There are very strict rules governing state visits, and Buckingham Palace and the police require the visiting nation to make a recce to the UK at least two months prior to the trip, after which the programme is cast in stone.

Scheduled into the programme was a daily walk for Mandela. This was because, following his release from prison in 1990, the President developed a habit of waking at 4:30 every morning and then taking a brisk stroll at 5:00 for an hour. With the beautiful parks in London, and the fact that Mandela would be staying at Buckingham Palace for part of the trip, the capital city was an ideal place for the President to slip into his daily routine.

Steyn had already told Mandela, upon his return from the recce in May 1996, that he could bring his running shoes and tracksuit. He had also informed the British security that his president enjoyed taking an early morning stroll. They were not exactly delighted at the thought of a 4:30 a.m. wake-up call, as 4:30 for the English is more like 2:30 a.m., as their day starts so much later. However, a special route was planned around St James's Park as this is near the Dorchester Hotel where Mandela would be staying for the first night.

After the official welcome he would then be transferred to Buckingham Palace. Mandela was due to arrive at midnight on 8 July. What the British security wanted to know was whether, given the President's late arrival, he would be taking an early morning walk on his first day in London. The President was arriving from Cameroon, following a hectic schedule at the bi-annual OAU summit. Steyn knew from experience that OAU summits were notoriously energy-sapping and constantly running late. He was sure that the President would be thoroughly exhausted. And so he decided to tell the British security that he thought the chance of an early morning walk was less than zero.

Less than zero for the average person maybe. But then President Nelson Mandela is not your average person. What Steyn did not count on was the fact that Mandela had slept throughout the plane journey from Cameroon and arrived in the

UK (albeit at midnight) fresh and ready to rock and roll. (He always slept well on his jet, 'the Falcon' as it was known to PPU members, but Steyn was not yet aware of this.)

Not only was Mandela not the least bit tired but he'd remembered Steyn telling him that he would be able to continue his daily walks throughout his stay in London. And he had every intention of making the best possible use of this facility. He quietly informed Steyn that he would like to take his walk at 5:00 a.m. This was after the entourage had arrived at the Dorchester Hotel only at 11:50 p.m. with security finally knocking off only at 1:30 a.m., after the usual team briefing regarding the following day's programme. And even worse, the mortified British protection officers had not made arrangements to remain in the city overnight. Most of them lived an hour outside London and would end up getting little more than an hour's sleep before having to begin the new day – not a good way to start a four-day state visit. But such is the nature of the peculiar job of being a protection officer. A visiting president's wish is law and everyone was expected to report promptly for duty despite the fact that they would still be wiping the sleep from their eyes and battling to stifle their yawns.

The only one who was not bleary-eyed that early morning was the 77-year-old South African President. Quite accustomed after 27 years in jail to rising early, he'd asked Steyn to give him a 4:30 a.m. wake-up call. The President was sleeping in the massive Presidential Suite; his daughter Zenani occupied one of the adjoining rooms, and Steyn the other.

At 4:30 a.m. sharp Steyn rose. He peered cautiously around the door into the massive Presidential Suite, in the centre of which was a huge extra-length bed, but the President was nowhere to be seen. Steyn stepped a little further into the room as the bed was partially obscured. There in a tiny corner of the massive bed lay the President, flat on his back with the barely disrupted bedding pulled up to his chin. A gentle tap on his shoulder was all it took to wake him and then he was up, into his tracksuit and ready for his morning stroll.

Professional as ever, the full security contingent was on time and ready for action. But as the day wore on, if anyone had looked closely, they would have seen the bodyguards looking more than a little worse for wear. One lucky photographer had been tipped off and managed to snap a grinning president in full stride, complete with a red London bus in the background – a picture emblazoned across that morning's tabloids.

The rest of the day was taken up with a full ceremonial arrival, including a street parade with a horse and carriage ride along The Mall from Horse Guards to Buckingham Palace. *One of my favourite photographs of the President is of him and the Queen, both smiling, Madiba waving to the vast crowd, as their carriage approaches the Palace. It hangs proudly in my lounge – a treasured memory.*

At this stage of the visit, Mandela had been fully ensconced in Buckingham Palace, his luggage and personal effects conveyed from the Dorchester to the Palace by efficient palace officials during that morning's ceremonial arrival and under the watchful eye of one of Steyn's men. It is no secret that Queen Elizabeth II has a soft spot for the South African President. For the next three days Mandela continued his tradition of rising early; and on one of the three mornings that he and his delegation slept in Buckingham Palace, he took his early morning walk around the palace gardens. *We used the private door to the gardens ordinarily utilised by Her Majesty, past the corgis' water dishes and blankets.*

The palace itself is massive, with a staff of more than 600. The passages are lined with huge, ornately framed oil paintings of members of the royal family spanning centuries. Then there are other extremely valuable paintings – so many that the spare ones are kept in a basement and rotated on a two-yearly basis. There is an entire staff component dealing exclusively with the artwork at the Palace – making sure it's catalogued and valued regularly.

The staff is impeccably behaved, adopting the maxim of being neither seen nor heard. But even these well-mannered and carefully chosen staff members could not resist the allure of

President Nelson Mandela. And many of the younger maids would hide behind the large drapes near the entrance to Mandela's suite of rooms, the Belgian Suite, just to catch a glimpse of him. On one occasion he caught them out and in true Madiba style called them over to greet them. One of them, however, had brushed up against a flower arrangement and had a smear of yellow pollen over her starched white pinafore. She was absolutely devastated and refused to come out even though Steyn urged her saying, 'He won't mind, he probably won't even notice.' But so great was her respect for Mandela that she missed the chance of a lifetime rather than be seen with a marked pinafore.

In addition to the maids, Mandela also had his own valet, butler and footman. They would wait for him at the entrance to the Belgian Suite, on call 24 hours a day. The President was constantly amazed that every time he entered or left his suite, there they would be. In fact they would only knock off when he had retired for bed and indicated he didn't require anything more.

So impressed was Mandela that he made history by becoming the first (and probably only) visiting head of state to request a photograph with the staff of Buckingham Palace. The entire staff component was assembled on the back steps of the palace garden; a sight never before seen in the stiff, starched palace environment.

Outside the comforts of the Palace, however, the President faced a tough schedule. First up was afternoon tea with the Queen Mother at Clarence House, followed by the centuries-old traditional British welcome accorded heads of state. It is a short but very formal, unique ceremony. So unique, that protocol forgot to brief the President.

The Lord Mayor of Westminster reads a special welcoming speech at St James's Palace (which adjoins Clarence House), the visiting head of state responds and then there is a ceremonial exchange of the actual written copies of the speeches. It has been so since time immemorial.

As the South African presidential party moved towards their cars at Buckingham Palace, Steyn asked the British appointed number one bodyguard, Stanley Downey, whether he had Mandela's speech. (Number one always carries the speech in the car in case the President wants to go over it *en route*.) He replied that he did not, so Steyn pressed the secretary at the time about it. Her response was that a speech was not needed for this engagement. But he felt sure it was, as they had gone over it in the recce visit months before. The secretary was confused, thinking that Mandela was only going to have tea with the Queen Mother, for which he did not require a speech. Same venue, two different engagements. Steyn pushed her on the matter and she must have had a moment of doubt. She told Steyn the speeches were all on her bed.

He ran back into Buckingham Palace as the convoy departed. *Sure enough there they were in 'Office of the President' folders. Each speech was marked separately in black koki pen. I grabbed the 'St James's Welcome Ceremony' folder and ran.* Fortunately St James's is very near Buckingham Palace. Up The Mall, first left. On the way, a British Special Branch car stopped for him. It had been sent back by the British number one, Downey. Steyn arrived just as Mandela was entering the room and surreptitiously handed the speech to a very relieved presidential secretary, who by then had probably checked her programme and realised that the speech was indeed required.

At the end of the speeches, the Lord Mayor handed his beautiful leather-bound copy to Mandela and put out his hand to receive the President's copy. Not having been properly briefed, Mandela didn't have a clue as to what he was supposed to do. The Lord Mayor requested a copy of the speech and the President handed it over.

So this ancient tradition was respected and the Lord Mayor's office now boasts a copy of President Nelson Mandela's speech in enlarged print form on plain white paper, complete with Mandela's amendments in his own hand above the typed text. Instead of leather binding, the speech is in a cardboard folder with black pen on the outside. It will probably end up being a collector's item in due course!

The contrast between the British love of the formal and Mandela's far more relaxed style was to repeat itself over and over again on this visit. But perhaps it was nowhere more starkly illustrated than on the occasion when he was made a Freeman of the City of London. It was a particularly great honour as the last serving head of state to receive the freedom of the city was a Chinese leader some 350 years ago.

The ceremony took place at the Guild Hall. This stone mansion in the middle of the city is a famous historic landmark, having survived both world wars. On arrival at the Guild Hall, a somewhat pompous guard of honour, wearing hot, heavy ceremonial garb, complete with long-shafted axes, welcomed Mandela. Everyone in the ceremonial guard of honour was a celebrity – a billionaire or two, captains of industry, and so on. As the President proceeded through the ceremony he was briefed on what happened next and then finally, in an excruciatingly solemn ceremony, he was handed the key of the City. Now Mandela had received the key to many villages, towns and cities around the world, but never before had he encountered such formality. This was a far cry from the dusty townships of South Africa, which preferred to celebrate with song and dance.

The formal ceremony was followed by a black-tie banquet at the Lord Mayor of London's residence, Mansion House. *As stunning as Buckingham Palace is, it's got nothing on this residence which had just been renovated to the tune of 23 million pounds. It is absolutely beautiful, boasting an impressive art collection also valued at millions.*

The President, who in a rare moment of formality himself had dressed in a suit for the first ceremony, was shown to a private room to change into his black 'Madiba shirt' and trousers for the banquet. While he was dressing, he turned to Steyn and said in a tone of complete amazement after the day's events, 'You know, our cultures are totally different!'

A typical Madiba statement from someone who just doesn't need all the pomp and ceremony that so often surrounds him.

By contrast, the visit to Brixton was the complete opposite of all this pomp and ceremony. The decision to visit Brixton (a predominantly black neighbourhood in South London) was at the request of Mandela himself. During the advance recce by South African and British security, the area had been inspected with a fine-tooth comb and together they had gone over the plans several times to ensure that everything would proceed smoothly.

The plan was that Mandela would open a community centre initiated and funded by Prince Charles's 'Prince's Trust'. Once this was completed, the President would visit several projects in the centre and then exit into the road outside. Crowd barriers would be erected on both sides of the road and then Mandela, Prince Charles and the community centre director, Mel Milbourne, would walk down the road for about 100 metres, waving to the people and simply doing what the President loved best, mingling with the crowds. That was why he wanted to go to Brixton.

The security men had already identified one potential problem on the advance recce mission: there was not much space between the crowd barrier and a wall running up to a railway bridge on the far side of the road outside the centre. Essentially, there was only enough room for the President, Prince Charles and the community director, plus security, to walk in the road. This meant that the large delegation accompanying Mandela would go straight from the community centre to the waiting coach and then head on to Trafalgar Square for the planned farewell ceremony at South Africa House. Prince Andrew was due to meet Mandela at Trafalgar Square and Prince Charles would depart in his own vehicle after the walk, for the rest of his day's programme.

Prior to the Brixton visit, a lot of work had been done in the area to ensure community co-operation. Brixton has a turbulent history and has often been the scene of violent race clashes between police and residents. During the advance recce, the Operations Inspector from Brixton police station, Jeremy Savill, had anxiously informed Steyn that the local police had worked very hard to obtain a 'tenuous truce' with the community. He was concerned that if anything went wrong, an hour-long visit from Madiba could result in three months of community–police conflict. *I assured him that we'd had our fair share of police–community conflict in South Africa and I would do everything in my power to ensure the visit went smoothly. I shared his concern and was determined to show that it could be a success for both the police and the community of Brixton.*

Everything looked fine on paper, but as Murphy's Law would have it, it's usually the best-laid plans that go awry. The problem arose after the opening of the community centre. Instead of returning to their coach (a luxury bus to South Africans) as planned, the enthusiastic delegation accompanying Mandela decided that they too wanted to share in some of the limelight and continued walking behind him and Prince Charles. A very concerned Steyn suggested to one of the palace officials, Lieutenant-Colonel Anthony Mather, that he should urge the delegation to get back into the coach or run the risk of a serious security breach. The uptight British official brusquely informed Steyn that he knew his job and that this was not the first state visit that he'd worked on. *Well, I was firmly put in my place. And not being my direct area of responsibility I concentrated on the President, as he most definitely was.*

But Steyn's gut instinct was right. The euphoric people of Brixton observed this huge snake of humanity walking down the road behind Mandela. They assumed that this was part of the crowd and that they were free to join in. *For the first and only time in my life I witnessed British police losing control of the situation.* There was no traditional British reserve here. People started jumping over the crowd barriers and storming Mandela.

Looking to his side, Steyn could see that the Brixton police were starting to panic and there was still a long way to the spot where it had been agreed that Mandela would get into his car. It was time for one of those split-second decisions. Only one vehicle had managed to get through the crowds. It happened to be one of the Queen's high-top Rolls-Royces that had been placed at the disposal of Mandela for the duration of the visit. The security back-up car and all other vehicles, including Prince Charles's Jaguar, were simply unable to get anywhere near Mandela. *I told Madiba that we had to evacuate as the crowd was becoming unmanageable. There was no choice but to put Prince Charles in the Rolls as well, as his vehicle was stuck way behind, in the wild crowd.*

Mandela's official companion on this trip was his daughter Princess Zenani Mandela-Dlamini, who had also been trapped in the confusion. *I shouted to one of the Bobbies, 'That's the princess, bring her to the car.' The Bobby grabbed her and pushed her towards the Rolls-Royce. Now that we had the three principals in the vehicle we could start moving forward.* But by now the crowd was totally out of control. South African and British protection officers were physically throwing people away from the Rolls-Royce as they tried to pull the doors open. Police on horseback moved in next to the car and this still didn't stop the seething mass of people. Many had their feet trampled as they deliriously tried to reach their hero.

Slowly the protection officers started gaining a semblance of control. The motor cyclists of the Special Escort Group (SEG) had by now managed to fight their way through the crowd. In a rather un-British manner they signalled to the bodyguards on foot to jump on the back of the motor cycles. Most of them did, ensuring a scene never witnessed before or since on a state visit in London! But Steyn remained running alongside the door of Mandela's Rolls-Royce until he was sure that the vehicle was moving faster than a running pace. The only problem was that now he, together with colleagues Siphiwe Mkhize and Frank Armstrong (now head of Tony Blair's security detail), were all stranded.

What followed was exactly like a scene from the movies. They stopped the first car that passed, a Renault 5, piled into the back and ordered the woman driving the vehicle and her boyfriend to 'follow that Rolls!' They were in a state of shock but gamely shouted back, 'How far?'

'To Trafalgar Square if necessary,' Steyn replied.

'We don't have enough petrol.'

'We'll buy some! Don't worry.'

In fact, Steyn had absolutely no idea how far they would need to go. This was not his country and the rules of the game were very different. *I started thinking what we would do if a similar situation had occurred back home in South Africa. I knew that probably the first plan of action would be to divert the cars to the nearest police station.* Steyn had been provided with a two-way radio by the British Special Branch. It was time to put it to the test. First he asked the woman driving the 'hijacked' car where the nearest police station was. Kennington was the reply.

Fortunately the 'hijacked' Renault was close enough to the Rolls-Royce to ensure communication. *I turned the radio on and suggested to Stanley, who was in the car with Madiba, that we divert to Kennington police station. He then put out a radio message to all police agencies in the area that this is what we had done.* The unconventional royal presidential vehicle was literally only half a kilometre from Kennington and by the time the Rolls-Royce had reached the police station, the little Renault was right behind them!

Steyn hastily thanked the woman who'd driven them there and rushed into the police station, asking for the station commander. *When he appeared I introduced myself and told him that I had President Nelson Mandela and Prince Charles behind me. I suggested that we go into his office and sit down in true British fashion and have a cup of tea, while we waited for the rest of the convoy to assemble out of the confusion we had just left behind. Well, he was gobsmacked and couldn't get a word out. But by that time Madiba was right behind me and his eyes could confirm what he thought his ears had heard. This was no practical joke!*

Mandela was of course completely unfazed and in fact was actually enjoying himself, making sure he greeted everyone in the police station, just as he would have done in South Africa. Prince Charles on the other hand was absolutely mortified. This kind of bungling did not go down well with the stiff upper lip, traditional Brits. He seemed convinced that he was responsible for the diplomatic blunder of the year. *He looked so distressed that I said to him, 'Your Royal Highness, please don't worry about this. The President is totally used to this sort of thing.' But he was not satisfied and hesitatingly asked, 'Are you sure?'*

Quite sure!

However, once the Prince saw how at ease Mandela was he started to relax a little. Apart from the loss of face for the British, the rest of the trip was uneventful and, in fact, the presidential party was only 15 minutes late for its next stop at Trafalgar Square for the final farewell.

I often wonder who that young lady was that helped us with her Renault 5 and whether she knew that it was President Mandela she was following! I hope she reads this book one day! Many British protection personnel that I bump into even now, years later, tell me that "that day in Brixton" is still part of their training curriculum; complete with video evidence.

The last goodbye from the UK was in fact quite an emotional event. It took place at South Africa House. Once the scene of militant and daily anti-apartheid demonstrations, it was now the property of the new Mandela-led government. And the man who had been at the centre of many of those protests now found himself walking through the entrance of a building that had once been the focal point of the hatred of the world.

Rounding off then what had been a very enjoyable trip for Mandela, he arrived at Trafalgar Square, which was packed with people once again desperate to catch a glimpse of the world-famous leader. *Madiba first walked through the crowds (all behind crowd barriers!) and then entered South Africa House. I will never forget appearing on the balcony with him. Although I was 'hiding' behind one of the pillars on the balcony, I still had a very good view of the crowds and it is a memory that I will take with me to my grave.*

FRANCE

After the high-profile and immensely successful UK trip, an increasingly exhausted President Mandela was supposed to return home on 13 July 1996. But as he was already in Europe, it was suggested that he made a quick detour via Paris for the Bastille Day celebrations on 14 July. The plan was to rest for the whole day in the country's spectacular capital on the 13th, and then attend the ceremony the next day. But the French were already miffed that they had become a poor second to the UK regarding a visit by Mandela. And not wanting to be outdone in any way, insisted on a four-day visit with all the pomp and ceremony afforded the South African President in London. *Such taxing demands on the President's time would never have happened later in his presidency. Once he had Graça Machel by his side, she made sure he said 'no' to certain engagements and would not tolerate excessive demands on his time. Madiba, on the other hand, found it extremely difficult to say 'no'.*

But while French noses may have been a little out of joint over the apparent favouritism afforded their British neighbours, the welcome extended to the President was as warm as it was grand. In fact so much so, that here too the French security lost control of the crowds. Only this time it wasn't in the rough and tumble of the Parisian streets, but in the contained environment of the official presidential residence, the Elysée Palace. Mandela was the guest of honour at an exquisite and stylish banquet here, attended by about a thousand of the cream of French society. But even the upper crust of French society could not contain themselves in the presence of the world's most famous political prisoner turned president. As he arrived, hysterical guests overwhelmed the President, pushing and shoving each other out of the way in their bid to win the privilege of greeting him. Even French President Jacques Chirac was forced to join the fray. By then the French security had lost complete control and the South Africans had to step in, in a bid to restore order. A frustrated Chirac joined them shouting out commands and acting like a star bodyguard as he pushed away elegantly clad men and bejewelled ladies!

The bodyguards were used to this by now and ended the evening completely unfazed. But their duties were not quite over yet. When they arrived at the official guesthouse, the Hotel De Marigny, they found Mandela's Director General Professor Jakes Gerwell in the main bedroom, called by Madiba because of a problem with the mattress. He asked the bodyguards to help him place the mattress on the floor. Just for that first night, the President slept on the floor amid the dazzling luxury of French hospitality.

But ever the diplomat and not wanting to offend his hosts, he had his bodyguards put the mattress back on the bed in the morning! And as had become customary, he would then proceed to make the bed himself. *Whether it's in a deluxe hotel, a beautiful palace or a presidential guesthouse, Madiba makes his own bed every morning without fail. It's something he inherited from prison, and I guess old habits die hard.*

GERMANY

'Mandela overwhelmed by crowds.' 'Foreign security loses control of crowds at Mandela welcome.' It was headlines like these that were to dominate Mandela's visits abroad. By now the South African bodyguards had become experts at dealing with crowd control. And whenever they went on a foreign trip, one of the first things they would inform the host nation of was the need for extra measures and precautions to be taken when Mandela went on a walkabout in their cities. *Our experience was such that the President was sure to be mobbed. The Brits didn't listen and time after time we were fobbed off by the host nation's security forces, who abruptly informed us that they had co-ordinated many state visits and knew what to do.*

This too was clearly the attitude of Germany's super-efficient VIP protection unit. 'Never before had they lost control of a crowd. And they did not intend to do so during Mandela's visit,' says PPU protector Johan Scott, who accompanied the President to Germany. And certainly at the beginning of the trip in May 1996 everything went smoothly. It was German precision right up until the Brandenberg Gate. Here Mandela was supposed to walk through the gate and be picked up by his car on the other side. And it was here that things took a turn for the worse.

Barricades had been placed along the road because this was, of course, a huge tourist attraction. Unfortunately for the German bodyguards, they walked right into a fresh busload of tourists who turned out to be largely South African. As soon as they saw Mandela the crowd started storming him and singing the South African anthem and '*Shosholoza*'. The German security just froze. This wasn't supposed to happen and was not in the plan. Therefore they simply didn't know what to do. Once again, the South African bodyguards had to quickly take over and restore some order.

ITALY

In Italy the presidential party was faced with a problem of a very different nature. The visit went smoothly as Mandela was accompanied everywhere by impeccably groomed bodyguards. But the drama occurred at a formal lunch hosted by the Prime Minister. The 20 or so guests were treated to a typical Italian meal when the Italian Minister of Foreign Affairs began choking on a prawn. His red-faced wife was so embarrassed that instead of helping him, she began closing his eyes and turning him away from the table. All the time he was growing purple in the face and looked as if he was choking to death. On this occasion, Mandela was accompanied by Graça Machel's youngest daughter, Josina, who took stock of the urgency of the situation and, throwing stuffy protocol to the wind, screamed at the top of her voice, 'Doctor! Doctor!' Mandela's accompanying physician, Dr Charles Niehaus who was a guest at the lunch, seized the initiative, rushed over and performed the Heimlich Manoeuvre on the poor man, literally saving his life. The problematic prawn was propelled from the poor man's mouth and the lunch continued, but probably not as normal!

SCANDINAVIAN COUNTRIES

The Italian authorities may have suffered mild embarrassment over the choking incident, but this was nothing close to the series of hiccups that South Africa's protocol department experienced during Mandela's tour of the Scandinavian countries. They say that bad luck comes in threes. That certainly seemed to be the case on this trip. It all centred on the presentation of South African awards to the distinguished leaders and royalty of the host nations. It began in the Netherlands where staff forgot to bring South Africa's highest honour, The Order of Good Hope, Class One – Gold, presented only to heads of state. At the last minute, frantic officials realised their error and had the order hurriedly couriered to the local airport where Madiba presented it to Queen Beatrix on his departure instead of at the state banquet the previous evening.

Then it was on to Denmark and another mistake. Whenever Mandela is presented with an order by an incoming head of state on a visit to South Africa, he is required to wear that decoration to the state banquet held in his honour, when he reciprocates and visits that country. Well, on this occasion the wrong decoration was sent but fortunately few people were versed in South African etiquette and probably didn't notice. But the cherry on the top of this trio of slip-ups came in Sweden.

South Africa's Head of Protocol, John Reinders, was sitting in the lobby of the hotel when he saw an unknown woman walking out of the hotel door with The Order of Good Hope, Class One – Gold that was to be presented at the state banquet later that evening, under her arm! The honour is worth a lot of money and Reinders had consequently requested that the hotel lock it in a safety vault at reception. Reinders rushed up to this woman shouting, 'What are you doing? That's not yours!' Without even blushing, she calmly responded, 'Of course it is.' It turned out that she was trying to steal the award and had brazenly managed to get her hands on it by informing the hotel reception that she was from the South African embassy and had come to collect the order ahead of that night's special presentation ceremony! *I have no idea how John would have explained that to the President!*

LIBYA

Perhaps one of the most extraordinary aspects of Mandela's presidency was the manner in which virtually every country around the world courted him. However, his ability to span both East and West, including countries that had become pariahs to the rest of the world, was not always met with international approval. But Mandela did not seem to care. He was uncompromising in his support for those who had befriended the ANC during the dark days of apartheid. And in the end he was able to bestride both worlds triumphantly. This was nowhere more evident than in his relationship with Libya. And it was this relationship that was to trigger an international breakthrough in the longstanding impasse over what had become known as the 'Lockerbie disaster'.

But all that was in the future. For now the West could not see beyond the immediate. Mandela was consorting with the enemy. And Libya's Muammar al-Gadaffi was regarded by the West as an enemy on a par only with Iraq's Saddam Hussein and Cuba's Fidel Castro. The West, and the United States of America in particular, was vitriolic in its disapproval. Not only was Mandela befriending one of the West's most hated leaders, but he almost seemed to flaunt the friendship. It was this, more than anything else, that stuck in the craw of the United States.

As far as the United States was concerned, Libya had been outlawed since the Pan Am Flight 103 crash over Lockerbie in Scotland on 21 December 1988. All 259 passengers and crew members on board the plane were killed when it exploded in mid-air and burst into flames. A further 11 people on the ground were also killed in the disaster. To this day the bodies of 17 people are still unaccounted for – it's believed they were completely vaporised in the explosion. A total of 270 lives were lost in one of the most blatant acts of terrorism the world had ever seen. And a further 270 families were left shattered by an incident that would drag on unresolved for years to come. An entire town and nations around the world were left devastated as they spent a black Christmas grieving over the loss of their loved ones. Ironically South Africa's then Foreign Minister, Pik Botha, and an accompanying delegation were booked on Pan Am Flight 103. But as it turned out, they arrived at Heathrow airport an hour earlier than expected and were able to get seats on another flight to New York.

Libya was blamed for the crash and in particular two Libyan nationals were suspected by the West of having placed an explosive device on the plane. But Gadaffi refused to hand over the Libyan nationals for trial in Britain or America. And it was this steadfast refusal that had resulted in a bitter political impasse between the three countries for nearly a decade. The West had tried everything, including applying crippling sanctions against the country, but Gadaffi would not budge despite the immense suffering of his people and economy.

He would not budge – until Mandela worked his magic. Libya had been one of the African National Congress's staunchest allies during the evil days of apartheid. And anyone who attempted to dictate with whom South Africa should be friends could, in Mandela's own words, 'Go and jump in a pool!' In fact, he was to repeat that sentiment on many occasions, including at a joint media conference with President Bill Clinton in Cape Town in 1998. Mandela's persistence and loyalty eventually paid off.

It is now common knowledge that South Africa under the guidance of Mandela and his then Director-General, Professor Jakes Gerwel, managed to resolve one of the longest outstanding international disputes of our time. It is no exaggeration to say that South Africa was the key that helped unlock the door leading to the resolution of this most sensitive issue.

The two Libyans suspected of masterminding the bombing of the PanAm jumbo jet were handed over to an international tribunal in The Hague and Libya's leader, Muammar al-Gadaffi, was brought out of the cold. For their part in resolving this extremely delicate diplomatic impasse, Prof Gerwel and HRH Prince Bandar el Saoud, the Saudi ambassador to Washington, were decorated by Mandela. This was one of the last such ceremonies performed by the President, in Cape Town on 11 May 1999. *I would like to say a bit about Prof Gerwel or "Prof" as he was known to his staff. His appointment as Madiba's director-general shows good political acumen as well as sound judgement. I believe that no better man could've been chosen to be Madiba's director-general. So often prominent members of a high-profile politician's staff behave as if they are that politician. Prof was the perfect foil for Madiba. At no stage did he attempt to steal Madiba's limelight. He went about his duty in a quiet, dignified way, working incredibly hard in the background in smoothing the road for Madiba to perform on a very high-profile stage. A case in point is the Lockerbie issue, where he finished off what Madiba initiated and quite fittingly received the credit due for the role he played. I have tremendous respect for Prof.*

It all began with Mandela's highly publicised first trip to Libya towards the end of 1997. The visit was the centrepiece of a particularly busy schedule for the President. The itinerary included Egypt, Tunisia, Libya, Scotland, Morocco, Tunisia, and then back to Libya on his way home to Johannesburg. Such a punishing schedule, where numerous countries were visited together, had become the pattern, because too many countries wanted Mandela and he was simply running out of time in office.

Because the internationally applied sanctions against Libya included an air embargo, there were no flights to the country at that stage. So an incredibly elaborate plan had to be worked out to avoid a long and arduous journey by car to the country's capital, Tripoli. Following a meeting with the Tunisian President, the presidential party flew to Djerba, an island city on the northeastern part of Tunisia, the closest part of Tunisia to Libya. From there, the Tunisian Air Force flew the South African party to the Libyan–Tunisian border post, Ras-Ajdir, by helicopter. Here they were welcomed by Gadaffi's personal luxury bus for the two-hour journey to Tripoli. The middle section of the bus had been converted into a palatial bedroom complete with a plush double bed and bathroom *en suite*. At the rear end of the bus was a u-shaped sofa in the centre of which was a table. A small kitchenette was off to one side. Here a steward served tea, coffee, cooldrinks and the Arab refreshments of dates and nuts. The President was accompanied by Graça Machel on this trip and the couple started the journey by resting in the bedroom.

But at some point along the route, they were called to witness an amazing scene along the streets. The entire route was lined with thousands of Libyans who danced in the streets with anti-US and pro-Mandela placards. As the bus moved from village to village, this scene was to be repeated over and over. 'Mandela ignores the West and comes to Libya' was the theme. This was clearly a triumphant moment for this outcast nation. And they were richly rewarded as Mandela spent most of the rest of the journey standing next to the driver and waving to the ecstatic crowds.

On his arrival in Tripoli, the 'Brother-Leader' Muammar al-Gadaffi, resplendent in a brown safari suit, made a rare public appearance to welcome Mandela. The Libyan leader had pulled out all the stops in the red-carpet welcome and the entire diplomatic corps and cabinet were there.

After the ceremony the two leaders moved to a special tent for a media conference. Mandela and Gadaffi sat side by side on two huge armchairs as the media fell over each other in their bid to get close to the two men. There was total pandemonium as questions were shouted in Arabic. As the translator began to translate one question, several more would be shouted out. The South African media officer from Mandela's office was rendered absolutely useless. Gadaffi let this chaos continue for about five minutes then clapped his hands once, shouted a brief phrase in Arabic and the media scattered. *They literally ran away simultaneously. I don't know what he said, but it clearly sent the right message!*

Gadaffi also wanted to send another kind of message during Mandela's trip. The first official engagement during the stay was to the site of the United States bombing of Tripoli in 1985. It was here that the American bombers nearly managed to kill the Libyan leader and where Gadaffi lost a beloved daughter. The building has been left exactly as it was after the devastating explosions – even the bloodstains have not been removed. The only outside touch is a specially erected monument depicting a giant steel fist squeezing a US fighter plane – a reminder of how close Gadaffi had come to being assassinated.

And clearly the near hit-job has left its mark. Gadaffi was obsessed with thoughts of assassination. After this visit, it was finally time to rest and the presidential party was escorted to a large double-storey guesthouse. This was to be the first occasion Steyn would have to sit down and talk to his colleagues from the advance team about the President's schedule over the next few days. To his surprise he was informed that they had still not received an official programme from the Libyan authorities. And in response to any enquiries, his colleagues had simply been fobbed off with that most Arab of phrases '*Inshallah*' (God willing). It had been a case of: 'Is there an official schedule?' '*Inshallah!*'; 'Will we receive a schedule later today?' '*Inshallah! We'll come back to you.*'; 'Will there be a state banquet tonight?' '*Inshallah!*'. God willing – a phrase that covers every and any occasion. And frustratingly for the South African delegation, it was to become the theme of the Libyan trip. They were learning very fast. *The reality was that due to the paranoia over assassination attempts, nobody below head of state level could take any decision. The chief of protocol was just a liaison channel and had no authority to make any final decisions. In effect what happened in Libya was that they hijacked you for the entire time you were there. You didn't ever get to see a programme, you knew nothing of the travel arrangements. And you were lucky if you got enough warning ahead of state functions. It was a case of, 'tonight there's a banquet. The leaders will speak.'*

In fact the only leader who really spoke there was Gadaffi himself. He was the only person who knew from one day to the next what was really happening. Not even his personal body-guards would know where he was going ahead of a trip or which convoy he would travel in. He would literally only inform his staff as they were about to leave. There was always more than one convoy ready and he would decide in an instant which one to take. The driver would then finally be briefed on the destination as the vehicles rolled out of the presidential residence. These convoys were led by Gadaffi's security. The men worked in v-neck safari suits and looked every bit the part. Sullen, muscular and in their late thirties or early forties, they did not give an inch. In addition to the men, there were also the famous 'gazelles', female Libyan bodyguards who had a reputation for being even more ruthless than their male counterparts.

But while Libyan security had a reputation for being particularly brutal if need be, there was no real sign of this during Mandela's trip. The only hint of aggression came on the first evening as the bodyguards making up the advance party left their hotel rooms to go downstairs. They handed in their keys at reception but literally five minutes later one of them remembered he'd left something in the room. To his astonishment he was told by reception that the keys were no longer there. The men rushed upstairs and found their rooms full of heavy Libyan cigarette smoke. It was crudely obvious that the Libyan security had been going through their luggage. But this was an isolated incident. For the most part the Libyans had been briefed to be of assistance to the South Africans; and once again the bodyguards watched in awe as the Mandela name opened doors that had previously been firmly shut in South Africa's face.

One door that still had to be opened, however, was the one leading to a resolution of the 'Lockerbie disaster'. As mentioned earlier it was this trip that sowed the seeds that would eventually give fruition to a breakthrough in the matter. On the first day of the trip, the South African and Libyan delegations met for talks. After about half an hour of pleasantries Mandela requested an opportunity to talk to Gadaffi alone. It was just the two of them and a carefully selected interpreter. *It was at that moment that Mandela raised the question of Lockerbie. I know this because I was standing guarding the entrance to the tent. I heard him say, 'Now, about the Lockerbie question.' That was all I heard because the talk got a lot softer after that and it was never my place to listen in on any of the President's conversations.* The talks lasted for about two hours. Nothing much was said at this point to the media. But a few days later in Scotland, Mandela hinted that he'd spoken to Gadaffi about the matter, which he then raised with British Prime Minister Tony Blair. For the first time the suggestion was made public that Gadaffi was open to handing over the two Libyan bomb suspects for trial by an international tribunal in a neutral country, as opposed to in the United States or Scotland.

The day's successes were then celebrated in a traditional state banquet that only got under way at about 10:30 p.m. It is customary at these occasions for the leaders of the two countries to make a brief speech. Mandela was extremely tired, and in deference to the elder statesman Gadaffi said he would make a far shorter speech than usual. Gadaffi was famous for speeches that went on for hours, so everyone breathed a sigh of relief at this news. Well, were they in for a surprise! After awarding Mandela Libya's highest honour, Gadaffi spoke non-stop for about seventy minutes. A record, the bodyguards were informed. And no, not a record for the longest speech ever, but the shortest. Gadaffi had in fact planned on making a four-hour address, but had cut it dramatically short out of deference to Mandela. And so in true Madiba style, the President said that he had no other choice but to return to Libya on his way back from the Commonwealth Heads of Government Meeting (CHOGM) in Scotland and reciprocate this award, contrary to our policy up till then not to award Orders while on travel. Hence the two trips to Libya in less than two weeks. The twin visits, however, were reported in the media as having a far more sinister motive. It was believed that Mandela was returning to Libya to inform Gadaffi of his talks with Britain's Tony Blair and, in particular, the media speculated that Lockerbie was high on the agenda. Nothing could have been further from the truth.

Mandela planned on making the briefest of stops in Libya to present the Order after Scotland. He informed his staff that there would be no media conferences after the ceremony, at the conclusion of which he wanted to leave immediately. But the Libyans had other plans; and while Gadaffi was receiving the Order from the President, his staff were preparing for the two heads of state to once again partake of their usual dates and tea, followed by a press conference. A room was prepared next door for this massive press conference. On seeing this, the South African bodyguards went to the room and shut the door firmly so that the media would not see Mandela leaving. Gadaffi signalled to the President to go inside, but Mandela insisted that now was not the appropriate time. A huge scuffle between the Libyan and South African bodyguards then ensued as the South Africans attempted to keep the door to the press conference room firmly closed. Mandela was spirited out of the room to his waiting car only to be told later that his media spokesman, Tony Trew, had lost his shoe in the bun-fight – a small price to pay for what was to become one of Mandela's most high-profile international success stories.

SCOTLAND

The timing of the Libyan trip could not have been more awkward from a political point of view. Mandela went straight from Libya to Scotland to attend CHOGM. The memories of the Lockerbie plane crash were still fresh in the minds of many Scottish people. With the benefit of hindsight and the knowledge that the impasse over Lockerbie has been successfully resolved, it may be that Mandela deliberately planned it this way. But at the time it looked like political suicide to many observers. But they had not counted on one thing: that famous Madiba Magic.

Mandela was not spared initially, walking into a hostile media environment, which included families of the Lockerbie victims. And at the first CHOGM reception he attended, Mandela was accosted by a man with a huge lapel badge reading 'UK Families Flight 103', demanding to know what Mandela had discussed with Gadaffi and whether there was ever going to be justice for the Lockerbie victims' families. There was no security allowed at this reception, but Steyn had managed to gain access. *I felt I would have to intervene as the atmosphere was so tense, but Madiba, in that disarming manner of his, was able to calm the situation.*

Later during the Scottish visit, one of the British protection officers commented on the 'stupidity of coming to Scotland directly from Libya'. *Hindsight is, of course, a perfect science, and I hope that my British colleague now has a better understanding of President Mandela's razor-sharp political acumen.*

Mandela spoke to some members of the families and won their respect and support. By then he'd raised the matter with Gaddafi and was ready to talk to Prime Minister Blair. *He had great faith in Blair's reasonableness and it was here that the real seeds were sown that would lead to the final Lockerbie resolution.*

It was not all hard work on this Scottish visit either. Unlike the hectic and disorganised pace of the OAU summits, CHOGM, which also occurs every two years, is characterised by a traditional retreat, usually on the Sunday of the meeting. This time it had been organised at St Andrews, the 'Home of Golf' and of the Royal and Ancient Golf Club. The venue was The Old Course Hotel, which was available only to CHOGM delegates. *So you would see some of the younger heads of government enjoying a round of golf on the hallowed grounds where some of the world's most brilliant and best-loved golfers had cast their spell.*

Blair's spin doctors were of course keen not to miss out on a golden media moment and used the occasion to set up a special photo session with Blair and Mandela. The two leaders were captured strolling arm-in-arm outside the hotel with the 18th fairway and clubhouse of the Royal and Ancient in the background. *Blair's media people squeezed every iota of mileage out of the photo op. This was in contrast to Madiba's media people who were fairly relaxed at the best of times. I mean, how do you raise Mandela's media profile! Even at its lowest point it was sky-high. You just didn't have to try. But it was interesting to observe the real world where even prime ministers compete for media space and have to try just that bit harder. A moment with Mandela captured on film and video was worth its weight in gold to Blair, or any other world leader for that matter.*

For the main part of the conference, the presidential delegation was put up at the Caledonian Hotel in Edinburgh. Here the Scots went completely overboard, almost outdoing the Americans with security measures. Even Mandela's security men were searched over and over again, despite having the necessary security passes. *It was ridiculous. When I entered the hotel with Madiba, I was granted 'free access', but if I popped out for five minutes and came back in by myself, I would have to be thoroughly searched! Sounds almost Irish!*

RUSSIA

It was a visit that almost never happened. Russia had been on President Nelson Mandela's agenda since his inauguration in 1994. But it kept being postponed due to the troubled political climate in the region and Russian President Boris Yeltsin's persistent health problems. But in the end Mandela was duty bound to visit a country that, although no longer communist, in the days of apartheid had been one of the ANC's most significant international champions.

True to his style, Mandela was determined that the visit would encompass both the present and the past. He was insistent on visiting Lenin's mausoleum. However, he was to encounter strong opposition from Yeltsin, who wanted nothing to do with his country's communist past. Given Mandela's profile, a visit to Lenin's mausoleum would certainly attract media attention. And the last thing Yeltsin needed was a world-famous icon like Mandela resurrecting the memory of a man who symbolised principles he believed were long dead and buried. Mandela's Chief of Protocol, John Reinders, explained this reluctance on Yeltsin's part to his president, who assured him that he would take up the matter up with Yeltsin personally. However, as it turned out, a diligent Russian protocol officer who overheard this conversation spared him the trouble. He informed Reinders that the mausoleum 'is not open today; but it would be open tomorrow!' Just enough time for a security recce mission and to put the necessary arrangements in place befitting a presidential visit.

The bodyguards visited the mausoleum the day before the President's visit and were met by a very stiff and formal Commander General. He laid down the law: no mobile phones, no recording equipment, no talking and everyone had to walk 'very softly and slowly.' There was only one route – 25 steps down, 5 steps up and there lay Lenin. Then the presidential party would leave via a specially arranged exit.

Mandela was duly briefed of the conditions surrounding the visit and went ahead with it the next day. At this stage Mandela was an 80-year-old man who needed assistance down the stairs to where Lenin lay. On arriving there he turned to the Commander General and casually asked, 'How long has he been lying here?' A few raised eyebrows and then the Commander General answered very softly hoping to get the message across that loud talking was not tolerated. It had no effect as Mandela simply pressed ahead saying, 'I can't hear you!' This went on, back and forth several times until the Commander General was faced with two options: either to let this talking continue endlessly or end it once and for all with one very loud answer. Needless to say he chose the latter.

But when it came to speaking loudly, Mandela was completely overshadowed by Yeltsin. Mandela's Director-General, Professor Jakes Gerwel, had warned the President that Yeltsin had a rather uncomfortable manner of conducting bilateral talks. He would issue instructions, commands and opinions very loudly in Russian, daring anyone to defy him. His interpreter would then try to couch these words in more politically discreet, diplomatic language. Not even Madiba escaped these vociferous bellows and they were a huge source of amusement to the South African delegation.

Diplomacy was also required when it came to Russian food. Says Zelda la Grange: 'I went out of my way to get him South African food, which was difficult with the Russians not speaking English. After the first attempt from their side, he said he wanted real Russian food and he was happy with it. Thereafter, he was stuck with it.'

NEW YORK

From east to west Mandela had friends everywhere. And despite his Libyan connections, one of his staunchest allies was United

States' President Bill Clinton. Ironically though, it was Mandela who would eventually prove the loyal friend, sticking by Clinton throughout the Monica Lewinsky sex scandal that plagued his second term of office. The same commitment to people that would not allow him to brush off Muammar al-Gadaffi also extended itself to Clinton in his hour of need.

Mandela's first trip to the United States as president took place towards the end of October 1995. Clinton is famous for his natural charisma. Like Mandela, he is clearly a people's person; more at home 'pressing flesh' than in political boardrooms perhaps. Those who work closely with him say he draws people to him; crowds flock around him eager to shake his hand and he bowls them over with his charm.

Well whatever Clinton has, it certainly cannot match Madiba's magic. This was nowhere more evident than during a massive state banquet arranged in Mandela's honour.

The President was in New York to attend the 50th anniversary of the United Nations. It was billed as the biggest security operation in the history of the world with 182 heads of state in Manhattan at the same time. Together the security protecting these world leaders amounted to well over 3 000 people.

This banquet was hosted by Clinton, who stood in the ballroom greeting his distinguished guests. Many of them were seated by the time Mandela arrived, while others were still pouring into the foyer. Imagine Clinton's astonishment when the room he was in was suddenly completely deserted. As Mandela arrived, these cool, sophisticated, well-travelled heads of state were instantly star-struck and literally rushed out into the foyer to greet this international icon. Clinton was virtually ignored and left waiting in the ballroom while his more famous counterpart was showered with praise and good wishes! But as was to become customary, none of this went to Mandela's head and he carried on with his simple daily routine unaffected by the hype around him.

This included getting up at 4:30 every morning for his 5:00 walk. Of course New York's Central Park was the perfect place for this. Fortunately his protection team had already gone over the route. They informed the American Secret Service that the President would walk on his first morning in New York. 'No problem, we'll report for duty at 7:30 a.m. then,' was their efficient response. This of course drew much laughter from the South African contingent who informed the dismayed Secret Service agents that the President would walk no later than 5:00 a.m. and often left earlier than that. Sure enough the Secret Service men reported for duty punctually the next day, kitted out in the latest running gear complete with brand-new running shoes (and their traditional earpieces).

The media had been invited, but arrived at 4:55 a.m. and found to their surprise that the President had already left fifteen minutes earlier. By this time the head of the American Secret Service had asked the South Africans where the President intended carrying out his exercise programme. 'Central Park,' they were told by the South African planning officer, Des van Rooyen. 'Well then you will have to lead the way,' the astonished South Africans were informed. This Secret Service detail was in fact drawn from all over America due to the huge number of heads of state and had never worked in New York before! So in the end it was a South African PPU officer, who had spent no more than a few days in New York, that was forced to lead the contingent of US/SA bodyguards on their route through Central Park, with all the Secret Service agents *behind* Mandela!

The walk was pretty uneventful until the last few minutes. It was at this point that Mandela encountered a street bum, sleeping on one of the park benches. (A huge clean-up operation had preceded the UN celebrations and most of the city's beggars had been cleared off the streets for the duration of the event. But obviously this one had slipped through the net.) This, of course, was right up Mandela's alley. To the absolute horror of the American security detail, the President deviated from his course and made as if to go over and greet the man. 'Bear in mind that it was still pitch dark at this stage and the increasingly nervous US security officials tried to stop him,' says van Rooyen. Words went back and forth between the two delegations. 'Mr President, Sir, we have to ask you not to go over there,' was the Americans' nervous request. 'It's fine, he's used to this,' came the relaxed South African response. 'Please, Mr President, do not go over there,' twanged the Americans even more nervously now, their busy Mag-lite torches scouring the surrounding bushes. 'It's fine,' said the increasingly irritated South Africans. This went back and forth for a while with the Americans eventually relenting and one lucky street beggar having the visit of a lifetime! Says Sam Shitlabane, 'This later elicited the surprised response from Madiba, "These Americans are strict." '

This more laid-back approach to life characterised much of Mandela's stay in New York. Now, New York's traffic is unbearable at the best of times. One can only imagine then the chaos that was caused by having the motorcades of 182 heads of state in the same city at the same time. It was only natural that there would be some serious traffic jams. Mandela's turn to be caught in one of them came as he was being driven to the Norwegian embassy one morning. His convoy became entangled with that of President Bill Clinton, which was travelling on the same road but in the opposite direction. This caused Mandela's convoy to come to a complete standstill in the middle of the very busy, very crowded 6th Avenue, Manhattan, as the local police understandably gave precedence to their president. Growing increasingly bored with the wait and ever concerned about being on time, Madiba looked at his watch, jumped out of the car and said to his bodyguards that in order to be on time they would have to walk. *Why the Secret Service didn't have the limo's doors locked is inexplicable. But the President was outside his vehicle before anybody could do anything to prevent it.*

Imagine the shock on the faces of hardened New Yorkers as they saw Mandela suddenly walking right next to them. It wasn't long before, like bees to honey, Mandela had attracted a huge crowd around him. Ignoring the frantic cries of his bodyguards to get back in the car, Mandela then walked in the middle of the road followed by hundreds of people chanting 'Viva

Mandela' and other such slogans. 'It made our work very difficult,' says Steyn's colleague, Des van Rooyen, 'It's almost as if he doesn't realise how famous he is. As soon as he gets out of a vehicle, it doesn't matter whether it's New York, Paris or Timbuktu, everyone knows him and they can't resist rushing up to him and trying to touch or greet him. It took us five years to "train" him, but even then he would still break ranks often enough to give us near heart attacks.'

Another heart-stopping moment in New York came in the last few minutes of the presidential visit. The presidential party was busy checking out of the Plaza Hotel in New York to catch a plane back home when Mandela asked where his daughter Zinzi was. (At this stage Mandela was separated from Winnie Madikizela-Mandela and had not officially announced his relationship with Graça Machel. His daughters often accompanied him as official companions on state visits.) The shocked bodyguards suddenly realised they'd forgotten to inform her to come downstairs and Sam Shitlabane frantically rushed back to the room to do so.

Mandela was to return to New York three years later. Once again it was to attend a United Nations meeting. But this time the world came together to say farewell to the South African President. And once again the world gave him a rapturous reception. His presidency was nearly over and yet during that time, unlike so many other leaders, he had done nothing to tarnish his image as an international statesman. The United Nations General Assembly rose as one as he entered the building and gave him a standing ovation the likes of which might never be seen again. This was repeated at another Clinton-organised state banquet. While Mandela was being fêted by the world, Clinton was being carefully scrutinised by the international media and Kenneth Starr. This visit, in 1998, coincided with his Grand Jury testimony in the tawdry Monica Lewinsky sex scandal. It was during this extremely testing time for the US President that Mandela gave him his greatest gift, that of a very public endorsement. At a time when few would touch Clinton, Mandela stood by him in his hour of need, saying what a great president he was. 'Clinton was moved to tears as our leader spoke,' recalls South African Hermann Coetzee, a bodyguard who was watching the banquet. This was a moment touched with delicate irony: whereas once the US had harshly criticised Mandela for standing loyally by Libya's Muammar al-Gadaffi, the boot was now on the other foot and Clinton found himself basking in Mandela's reflected glory. In his hour of greatest need, Mandela had come through for him, ever consistent in standing by his friends and supporters no matter what their personal circumstances happened to be. *Typical Madiba, if he thought that someone was doing a good job, he would say so.*

Also, this gesture provided a poignant insight into just *who* the most powerful statesman in the world was. Politically, William Jefferson Clinton had to be the modern world's most powerful *president*, simply by virtue of the office he occupied. When it came to who the world's most influential *statesman* was, however, few would deny that that honour belonged to President Nelson Rolihlahla Mandela of the Republic of South Africa.

This support for Clinton was really a sequel to the US president's visit to South Africa six months earlier. Clinton visited South Africa in March 1998. And once again, just days before he was to depart on his great African safari, the Monica Lewinsky affair boiled over. Lewd details of the couple's adulterous sexual escapades made headlines around the world and appeared verbatim on the Internet. It became so embarrassing that Clinton actually telephoned Mandela about the South African trip. Steyn recalls taking the call from the White House while Mandela was in Qunu. *Clinton's presidential aides set up a time to phone back to discuss the upcoming visit as Madiba was resting when the first call came in. Clinton then telephoned to ask Madiba whether, given the scandal surrounding his presidency, it was still all right for him to come to South Africa.* Of course the famous Mandela loyalty came shining through as the elder statesman informed Clinton, 'We are all looking forward to your visit!' An interesting aside is that when Clinton visited South Africa, Mandela's connection with

Libya once again flared up, but this time the American President did not enter the fray and left the criticism up to political observers.

CANADA

Mandela's hectic schedule did not end with the second New York visit. Directly after a week of frenetic activity where he was literally inundated with visitors, including the legendary Mohammed Ali at his Manhattan hotel, the President was off again. This time to America's less flamboyant northerly neighbour, Canada. But all this was taking its toll on the ageing president. Now in his 80th year, Mandela was nearing the end of his presidency and was no longer able to cope physically with such demanding schedules: schedules that would often tire his bodyguards who, in some cases, were almost three times younger than him.

Madiba arrived in Vancouver absolutely exhausted. His protectors had already been informed of the President's condition and had arranged everything for him in his hotel room so that he could take a brief nap. But Mandela's head had hardly touched the pillow before he was up again to go downstairs to attend a formal luncheon meeting. This was a crucial mistake.

Hermann Coetzee, one of the South African bodyguards, recalls listening on his two-way radio and hearing sudden pandemonium in the dining room. Sam Shitlabane, the national commander, was urgently calling over his radio for a doctor. The medic who accompanied Mandela on this visit had slipped out for a few minutes to go to the toilet. Upon his return to his seat he saw Mandela standing at the podium sweating, breathing heavily and looking very ill. The President had just finished speaking, but he was so ill that he couldn't move and simply stayed put, holding onto the podium for dear life. The doctor acted very quickly and whisked Mandela up to his room while staff gathered outside, desperate for word that the President was all right. Rumours were now flying thick and fast and word was already out that Mandela had died. And before long Mandela's media officers were inundated with calls from journalists, even those back in South Africa, asking about the President's health. At this point the only people allowed into Mandela's room were his wife, Graça Machel, his Director-General, Jakes Gerwel, and the doctor. Everyone else, even close staff members, were kept out.

This of course only further exacerbated the situation and fuelled speculation that staff were being kept away because their worst nightmare had come true. Mandela was dead! In fact nothing was further from the truth. Although Madiba had looked very grim during the luncheon it turned out that he was just feeling faint because he hadn't eaten anything all day. Graça quickly organised a bowl of soup and he was all smiles an hour later. Of course the news had now gone around the world and it would take some time before the media would believe that Mandela wasn't on his deathbed.

In order to scotch speculation that the President was critically ill and to prevent the rand making another spectacular nose-dive, he actually got up a while later and attended a banquet that evening to prove his detractors wrong.

But the scare had done its trick. After this Graça took a much firmer hand, insisting that his schedule be scaled down. Mandela, however, was his own worst enemy and he would sometimes sneak out of his Houghton home with instructions to the staff to tell Graça he was around somewhere if she called!

The rest of the Canadian visit was pretty uneventful by comparison. Apart from the presidential health scare, Canada will be remembered as probably the only place in the world where crowds of onlookers actually obeyed security and did not storm Mandela when he appeared in public!

Although this says much for national discipline it is also perhaps an indictment – just a small one: if Nelson Mandela cannot excite you, what will?

COMMITMENT TO AFRICA

Mandela's commitment to Africa as a whole was clearly evident during his presidency. Apart from his numerous visits to

African countries, Mandela also played a crucial role in the Organisation of African Unity (OAU) and was elected Chairman of the Southern African Development and Economic Community (SADEC) in 1997. This followed the retirement from office of SADEC's first chairman, the highly popular Sir Ketumile Masire of Botswana. Consequently, in addition to his travels abroad, Mandela was also obliged to attend numerous OAU and SADEC summit meetings during the course of his presidency.

A constant source of irritation to the President was the complete lack of punctuality that characterised these meetings. Mandela was never late. And he liked to get in, get down to work and get the job done. Very often these meetings would be bogged down in tedious verbosity. Initially, when the meetings dragged on unnecessarily, he would simply leave early. But after he started getting a reputation for not staying to the end, he was forced to adjust his way of dealing with these meetings.

Gradually, his bodyguards learnt to read his body language, knowing there were times when Mandela just had to go but needed a gracious way out. *On one occasion, I walked in on a heads of state meeting at an OAU summit. You don't do something like that lightly. But this was different. The meeting had taken place on the last day of the OAU summit in Harare in 1996. It had hastily been arranged at the last minute in a hotel conference room. I think about five other heads of state were supposed to attend. The President had arrived for the meeting, and as was so often the case, he was the first one there. Some of the other heads of state didn't even bother to turn up. It was clear that this meeting was going nowhere and was fast becoming a damp squib.*

Steyn whispered to the presidential secretary that it was time to pull Mandela out of the meeting. *I could see from his body language that the Old Man wanted to leave. One of us had to walk in there and do it.* But she was too nervous so it was up to Steyn. *Taking a leap of faith, I walked in. One of the other presidents was speaking, so I said, 'Excuse me, Mr President,' and then turned to Madiba and said,*

'Mr President, please remember we have to leave soon as you have that special function in Pretoria at 5:00 p.m.'

There was no such function planned. But Mandela was so relieved, that he got up, offered his apologies and said his good-byes. *As he was boarding the plane I said, 'Tata, I hope you didn't mind me doing that,' and he just laughed and said, 'No, no that was good. You saved me!' All I'd really learnt to do was to read his body language. I knew he wanted to leave, because one of the presidents was simply waffling on* ad nauseum, *but he felt obliged to stay.*

During his presidency of SADEC, Mandela would often provide his counterparts with lessons in punctuality. On one occasion during a SADEC meeting in Malawi, Zimbabwean President Robert Mugabe arrived late. Mandela insisted on waiting for him and finally began the meeting two hours late. This meant that they would not be finished in time for supper, but to make his point the President insisted on working through the night until all the business had been completed. The exhausted group of leaders finally concluded matters at 1:00 a.m. the next morning when Mandela at last suggested that they break for supper!

During this particular trip to Malawi, South African protection officers were treated to one of the funniest sights ever witnessed on their wide-ranging travels throughout the continent. *One evening Herman, Scotty and John Reinders were driving into Blantyre to buy food. As they entered the city via its main traffic circle, they were greeted by a large neon sign reading 'Welcome to SADEC 1997' flashing on and off.*

Closer inspection revealed a local, sitting on a fold-out camp stool underneath the sign, turning the electric switch on and off to make the sign flash on and off!

THE GREAT LAKES REGION

This sprawling region in Africa – which comprises Uganda, Rwanda, Burundi and the Democratic Republic of Congo – was to become one of the most troublesome hot spots during Mandela's term of office and still keeps him busy today as he mediates in the Burundi civil conflict. While South Africa was getting on with the peaceful task of reconstruction and development, this region would periodically witness some of the worst atrocities ever committed on the African continent.

First there was the horrific genocide in Rwanda, which led to a mass exodus of refugees and gave rise to desperate conditions in refugee camps all over Uganda. Just when things seemed to be settling down, they started to flare up in what was then called Zaïre. Rebel groups led by Laurent Kabila were gaining ground and Mandela was called upon to mediate between the rebel leader and Zaïre's dictator, Mobutu Sese-Seko. One of Mandela's most highly publicised diplomatic efforts was his attempt to broker a peace deal between Kabila and Mobuto. It was important to hold the talks at a neutral venue. Negotiations were set to take place on foreign waters, namely aboard the *SAS Outeniqua*. This was a South African Navy replenishment vessel deployed in the Antarctic, which was moored in Brazzaville in the Congo. Mandela was literally only due to spend the day there, after which he would fly to Mowana Lodge in Botswana where Steyn and his advance team awaited. The talks were set down for 3 May 1997 and he would then spend 4 to 6 May at the Lodge, which is set on the Chobe River and is truly a piece of paradise with game aplenty. However, what the President did not count on was the obstinacy of the two men with whom he was dealing. They eventually finished on 6 May, and because he was not expecting to stay that long, neither he nor his delegation had taken sufficient clothing with them to sleep on the Outeniqua for three nights. Consequently, clothing and toiletries were flown up to Brazzaville.

First Kabila arrived, but Mobuto refused to come, so Kabila left – by which time Mobuto changed his mind and pitched up, so Kabila had to be called back. By this time Madiba was fed up and out of frustration sat the two men down and literally said, 'Now talk and sort this out.' In the end, however, whatever agreements were reached on that ship never really came to anything. Kabila still took the country by force, and Mobuto Sese-Seko died from cancer shortly thereafter.

Certainly Kabila rarely behaved with distinction on his visits to South Africa. On one occasion, while attending the Non-Aligned Summit (NAM) in Durban, he arrived hopelessly late for proceedings. It was hoped that with the presence of leaders from all the parties involved in the DRC crisis, talks could be held during the summit. Kabila not only arrived late, but refused to participate in negotiations. His only appearance in front of the media was scheduled to take place at a media briefing at one of the city's plush hotels. He kept journalists waiting for over six hours, until around midnight. They watched as bottles of Johnnie Walker Blue Label were spirited into the room. Eventually he showed his face but was so drunk he could barely string an intelligent sentence together. His aides took him straight to the presidential plane and he left for the DRC a few hours later.

MAPUTO

One of the favourite presidential destinations was of course the Mozambican capital of Maputo. It was here that Mandela went to visit the love of his life, Graça Machel. As the relationship developed and became more public, these visits became more frequent. The bodyguards, in particular, enjoyed these visits, as they were more of a holiday than real work. But there was one heart-stopping moment. Mandela was due to fly up to the small Mozambican village of Xilembene to meet Graça's family. (This was shortly before the couple married in secret. The family were called in to give the couple their blessing.) Xilembene is a tiny rural village and is certainly not on any known air route. A South African Air Force Oryx helicopter had been flown in specially to transport the President. But the problem was that upon arriving at the co-ordinates indicated by the planning officer as the spot for the landing zone, there was nothing but virgin African bush – no sign of even the tiniest of dwellings. (Co-ordinates are determined by using a Global Positioning System (GPS) which determines the exact latitude and longitude co-ordinates, using navigational satellites.) Without this back-up, the pilot was completely lost and began circling what looked like the middle of nowhere in the hope of finding a way out of the situation. Not having any knowledge of Mozambican air space, the South African Air Force pilots would rely totally on the PPU planning officer to provide them with the correct co-ordinates. Eventually the pilot was forced to land because by then the chopper was fast running out of fuel. He climbed out of the chopper and in frustration threw his helmet on the ground. By now the President, too, was getting a little irritated. Then suddenly out of the bushes a crowd of men carrying pangas appeared. They were extremely friendly but equally unhelpful as they couldn't speak a word of English and no one on board the chopper spoke Portuguese. Then suddenly out of this crowd of about a hundred locals, a man came forward and said in excellent Afrikaans, *'Hallo, hoe gaan dit?'* (Hallo, how are you?) It turned out that he used to work on a South African mine where he'd picked up his Afrikaans!

The pilot had been studying a map of the area, which the newly-arrived Good Samaritan took and turned around. He knew how to read it, but it had to be from his own perspective, and according to him these crazy South Africans had been looking at it the wrong way round! He pointed towards the south-west and said that if the President flew in this direction for about half an hour they should arrive in Xilembene! What other choice did they have? So the party duly did this, only to find nothing once again. Just before total desperation set in, one of the bodyguards heard the familiar scratching on his two-way radio in his earpiece. By flying in such a manner that the radio signal got better not worse, talking to the pilot all the while on his head-set, they managed to establish communication with one of the bodyguards already on the ground in Xilembene. They suggested he throw a smoke-grenade so that they could land, as the fuel situation for the pilots to return to South African soil was becoming critical. However, they were still 10 kilometres away – too far to see the first smoke signal. Eventually, by following the radio signal, they finally managed to land in the right place. Says Van Rooyen, 'The whole time your heart is in your mouth. Those guys could have got hopelessly lost. Or worse still, even crashed. And nobody wants to be around when disaster strikes on your shift.'

LOST IN AFRICA

Mozambique wasn't the only place that was difficult to navigate the President around in. The bodyguards were to get lost on a number of occasions, most notably in Africa, which, due to its poor infrastructure, was not the easiest continent to negotiate.

On one occasion the presidential bodyguards were driving to the Zimbabwean capital of Harare to await Mandela's arrival when they got hopelessly lost. One of their party said it would only take about seven hours and so they decided to drive rather than fly. The team left at two in the afternoon, got through Beit Bridge at 7:00 p.m. and then realised it was still another 545 km to Harare. *I was not impressed... We refuelled at Masvingo at about 9:30 p.m., tired and hungry (we'd been on duty since 6:45 a.m.), and then asked the petrol attendant for directions. 'Just go straight,' was his vague response. We travelled what appeared to be 'straight', but later stopped to ask somebody the way and realised we had gone in completely the wrong direction, ending up on the Mozambique border in Mutare! It was still another 365 km to the capital.* In the end they arrived in the early hours of the morning. The next time they visited Zimbabwe, they flew.

EGYPT

The Egyptian visit was part of that state visit that included Tunisia, Libya, Morocco and Scotland. Accompanying the President on this trip was Graça Machel – who now had the status of 'Official Companion'. For Steyn, keen to make a good impression on his boss's new love, the visit did not get off to a good start. Already Graça was becoming an integral part of Mandela's life and would perform those gracious tasks that fall to many a companion or wife. She had packed for Mandela and, because it was a particularly long trip, she had organised the luggage in such a way that some of the suitcases went to Egypt and Libya and a different set went to Scotland (where they would spend the longest period of time). Steyn had asked which of the suitcases went where, but somehow they had got their wires crossed and the wrong ones went to the different countries.

The net result was that Graça didn't have the clothes for the country she was visiting. Steyn was a bit nervous and fully expected to be at the receiving end of a flood of abuse. *Instead of throwing her toys out of the cot, which is probably what most women (and certainly every former first lady) would do when they discovered they had no clothes, she was extremely gracious and practical. She merely arranged with one of the ladies from our embassy to go shopping in Cairo for an outfit to wear to the state banquet. I really admired her for the dignified way in which she handled it. She certainly lived up to her name and handled the entire affair with grace. A far easier route to go would have been to blame 'the stupid bodyguard', but fortunately for me she didn't.*

After this initially bumpy start the trip turned out to be a great success and was one of the few occasions when the President managed to mix business with a little bit of pleasure. The presidential party was treated to a private light and sound show at the pyramids. *It was truly awesome. Both Madiba and Graça commented on what a special occasion it had been. It was something we'll all never forget. And it was really great to see the presidential couple doing something 'touristy' for a change, instead of just attending summits and conferences and seeing only the insides of hotels and airports.*

SAUDI ARABIA

Mandela made many trips to Saudi Arabia and other Arab countries such as the United Arab Emirates, Oman and Bahrain. *The difference between Saudi Arabia and other Arab countries is like chalk and cheese. Most of the other states are fairly secular, while Saudi Arabia is one of the strictest Muslim countries around.* If Mandela is accompanied by any of his female staff, they are required to dress in the traditional *abaya*, making them look a little like black phantoms. Even Graça Machel was forced to wear the black cloak and bow down to the oppressively sexist traditions surrounding women (which perhaps explains her reluctance to visit there). Mandela's personal assistant, Zelda la Grange, found to her detriment what defying the rules of the land could mean.

> 'From the moment we landed I wasn't allowed to go any-where with Madiba. And on one occasion when I was walking in a Saudi Arabian market, I removed the veil of my *abaya*. The *Mattawa* (religious police) started whip-ping at me with a stick, yelling, "Cover up, woman, cover up!" It was not like that all the time, and the Saudi hos-pitality knew no bounds.'

Prince Bandar, the Saudi ambassador to Washington is, by con-trast, far more Western in his dealings with women and was very fond of Zelda.

SECURITY AROUND THE WORLD
United States

While procedures and cultures differ from country to country, just like policemen and women around the world, presidential security teams have much in common, with very similar subcul-tures and often common terminology. Most of them refer to their jobs as 'baby-sitting'. The Americans have the reputation of being the most irritating. *I have to say that while I don't agree with their policy of putting hundreds of pairs of eyes and feet out there, I do envy their budget and they are good at getting the job done.* But while they may be good at getting the job done, they do tend to go over the top. During one visit to South Africa, for the Bilateral Commission chaired jointly by US Vice-President Al Gore and South Africa's then Deputy President Thabo Mbeki, they were completely out of order. Not only did they snarl up major national roads during peak traffic by blocking on-ramps to urban freeways so that their Vice-President could pass, they had the gall to order parliamentary staff out of their own offices because Gore was coming. That particular Security Detail Leader was actually fired after that trip.

United Kingdom

The British, on the other hand, are equally well trained, but they prefer to go the discreet route. They don't believe in putting so many bodies on the ground, but those who are there are the cream of the crop, all graduates, well-informed and good to work with.

Africa

In Africa, most protocol officers and the security teams behave like their principals. *Sir Ketumile Masire of Botswana's security team were great to work with as were the Mozambicans, Tanzanians, Ghanaians and Ugandans. By contrast Zimbabwean President Robert Mugabe's guys were extremely pushy, and as for the Togolese and the Nigerians, they were indescribable: impossible to work with. But I have to compliment the Namibians; their presidential convoy is the most impressive one I have ever travelled in anywhere in the world. Every vehicle was a brand-new black Mercedes Benz and spotlessly clean. The motorcade lent the necessary dignity to the President it was transporting.*

During a flash visit by General Abubakar we had to throw one Nigerian bodyguard out of the presidential residence in Pretoria, Mahlamba Ndlopfu. We have a rule that we do not allow foreign security into the President's house. If their leader is visiting the President, only his aide-de-camp or the most senior bodyguard will be allowed in. But neither of them can be armed. Now this chap insisted on entering with a gun even though the aide-de-camp was already there and even though he'd been thoroughly briefed prior to the visit. We told him that if he didn't leave we would have to use physical force. He said, 'Fine, go ahead,' and consequently we literally picked him up and removed him from the house.

This was to have an interesting sequel several months later. The Nigerian security swore to get their revenge when Mandela eventually paid a visit to Nigeria, saying, 'When you animals come to Nigeria, we'll be waiting for you.' Well, this duly happened. Mandela's team flew with him to Nigeria and arrived without the support of an advance team, whose flight had been cancelled in Amsterdam.

Well, they harrassed us from morning until night until the moment Abubakar shook hands with me. And the only reason he did this was that he'd given the President an extremely valuable gift, which Madiba had handed over to me. It was in a briefcase brought by the Nigerian leader. Madiba's instructions were not to let this brief-case out of my sight. Now Abubakar saw me carrying the briefcase and realised that the President trusted me, and thus came over to acknowledge me. Well, that handshake changed everything in the eyes of these security people, who were to treat us like gold for the rest of that trip and on all subsequent visits.

" ...

A true story as told by
Nelson Mandela

As you know, I spent some time on an island once. At one point we were told that a senior prisons official from Pretoria was coming to visit us and I was to be given an opportunity to address him. I made about two pages of notes in Afrikaans and then went over and over them. I then called two Afrikaans-speaking warders, put aside the notes and said I want you to listen to my Afrikaans and tell me how it sounds. After listening to me they said, 'Mandela, jy praat suiwer Afrikaans.' (You speak pure Afrikaans.) Puffed up with new-found confidence, I went to the office of this official the next day. I started addressing him and he listened patiently at first, but then I saw him begin to get uncomfortable. After a while he stopped me and said, 'Jong, jy moet liewer jou eie taal praat. Jou kennis van Afrikaans is baie sleg, en jou uitspraak baie swak. Jy klink soos 'n tokoloshe!' (Listen, you had better speak your own language. Your knowledge of Afrikaans is very bad and your pronunciation very poor. You sound like a tokoloshe!)

. . . "

5

Home is Where the Heart is

I am simply a country boy.
(Nelson Mandela on his rural roots.)

 evered by millions. Regarded as a legend in his own time – an icon and world statesman. All this and yet at heart Mandela is still (by his own admission) very much a country boy.

A PROUD ROYAL HERITAGE

A proud Xhosa with royal blood coursing through his veins, Mandela will still bow deeply to traditional Xhosa leaders – his chiefs and kings. And he has made sure that he has instilled the same deep respect among his grandchildren. This knowledge was also extended to his bodyguards – who on the frequent visits to Mandela's home village of Qunu would be educated about the President's roots and exactly how to behave in front of Xhosa royalty. *For example, the King of the Thembus does not shake hands. The first time I accompanied the President to see him, Madiba pointed this out to me before introducing us.*

Visiting royalty is something that Mandela spends a fair amount of time doing when he's staying in Qunu. He does so out of respect and despite the fact that the reigning King of the Thembus is years younger than he is. He's been dubbed the 'Rasta King' by Mandela's bodyguards because of the dreadlocked hair he sports. The education of the protectors has included a detailed history lesson on the royal Xhosa lineage.

Ask most of the bodyguards and they will be able to name Xhosa kings past and present. On one occasion as they were driving through Qunu, Mandela started relaying messages to Steyn over the police radio, 'Tell Rory that all these cows we are passing belong to the King ... this is the King's land from that mountain to over there ...'

The same respect afforded the kings in Transkei is of course carried over to city life. When for example the 'Rasta King' comes to visit Houghton, Mandela will ensure that all the traditional ways of paying respect are enforced. One day the King popped in to visit Mandela's eldest grandson, Mandla. Now, as mentioned, he sports dreadlocks and is very modern in most of his ways. So he thought nothing of bunking down with Mandla who stays in a set of rooms adjacent to the presidential house. However, Mandla thought it prudent just to inform Madiba that the King was visiting. As it turned out, it was a bad move. *I later said to Mandla that he should either have brought the King over, or said nothing at all because his grandfather's reaction was to be true to form: 'Have you given the King some breakfast? Where is he sleeping tonight? How can you treat the King this way? Please have him sit in the lounge so that I can greet him when I come downstairs!' The King of course was chuckling while Mandla related this story. But it was a typical reaction – indicative of Mandela's deeply ingrained respect for his culture and its leaders.*

This deeply ingrained respect for culture and tradition was also extended to the royalty of other ethnic groups. And it stood Mandela in good stead when he had to resolve tribal conflicts. In particular it assisted him greatly in dealing with people like Zulu King Goodwill Zwelethini who, prior to the 1994 election, was reluctant to co-operate with the ANC in KwaZulu-Natal. At that particular time the province was in the grip of political violence. He was an important factor in resolving the tension, as Zulu people, whether they were ANC or IFP, would unite together out of love for their King. One word from the King and it could easily have helped deflect an already out-of-control situation. But the King was seen to be biased in favour of Chief Mangosuthu

Buthelezi and the IFP (who at that stage refused to participate in the upcoming poll – another factor responsible for an escalation of the conflict). As it became clearer that the ANC was going to win a landslide victory in the election, Zwelethini was forced to assess whether he was backing the right person. The problem was of course money: for over two decades IFP leader and Bantustan boss Mangosuthu Buthelezi had controlled the purse strings. The King could not do anything alone. As the ANC began to make approaches towards the King, he gradually started to shift allegiances to the point that there was a breakdown in his relationship with Buthelezi. At this stage Mandela decided to intervene again. He approached the King and said he should make his peace with Buthelezi. At this point Zwelethini broke down in tears and said that he'd been kept in prison for twenty years by Buthelezi and had no desire to have anything to do with him. Mandela then approached big business to take over the King's finances, so that he could be truly independent from Buthelezi.

A LOCAL MEDIATOR

Mandela's love of the place of his birth is something he spoke of frequently during his term of office. Whenever possible, his doctors would instruct him to sneak away from his official duties and get some rest in the place that he loved so much. How much rest he actually got while he was in Qunu is a moot point because whenever he was there, he would become deeply embroiled in the affairs of the tiny village and the wider area. No sooner would he retire for a nap in the afternoon than one of the elders would be knocking at his door asking for assistance in resolving some local dispute. They didn't usually come to him as President, but rather as a respected and senior member of the local clan who had a duty to assist in the issues of the small area. It's almost as if they were unaware of the power of this international statesman. But this lack of fear on the part of the community when it came to asking their leader for help was obviously mainly due to Mandela himself, who retained a deep commitment to this tiny village and never put on any airs and graces while he was there. Even the local police would come to him with their problems and here this head of state would humbly attend a local grievances meeting – hardly the stuff of presidents, but an indication of the measure of the man.

The measure of the man was also displayed in his humility when it came to acting as a local community mediator. Remember that we are talking about a world leader who has been called on to help solve major international crises. There was, as is documented elsewhere, his biggest international success with the 'Lockerbie impasse'. And equally important, there were Mandela's attempts to bring peace to the Democratic Republic of Congo, which was in the grip of a devastating war. Similarly, he was asked to assist in resolving the decades-long civil war in Angola. And when war broke out in Kosovo and the international community labelled Yugoslavian President Slobodan Milosevic a war criminal and turned him into an international pariah – who did he turn to for help? Mandela, of course. Milosevic requested the President's intervention in the crisis that eventually led to NATO sending troops into Kosovo. (It was a request that Mandela wisely turned down, commenting at the time that it should be handled by European leaders, as it was a European conflict. Tough stuff, but all fitting work for a president and man of Mandela's stature.

Well, little did this same President realise just how useful his considerable and internationally praised mediation skills, together with his ability to affect genuine reconciliation, would be in his tiny home village of Qunu.

One day while resting in his home, an elderly woman from the village knocked on his door. She'd come to him with a huge problem. She explained that she'd had a huge fat chicken in her back garden that had disappeared a few days before. Since then she'd followed the trail to a neighbour, who she was convinced had stolen the bird, slaughtered it and duly eaten it. She was furious and wanted justice and revenge for this terrible crime.

Could Madiba please help? The President thought long and hard and eventually asked the woman how much the chicken was worth. 'Ten rand,' she responded. 'Fine,' said Mandela, promising to come back to her with a solution. He tracked down the errant neighbour and explained the problem. The neighbour had had no idea to whom the chicken belonged, as it had simply wandered onto his land one day. But after a long discussion he agreed to compensate the woman. He would repay her the monetary value of the chicken. Ten rand was duly handed over and, satisfied with his results, Madiba returned to the woman and proudly presented her with the money. She stared at it for a few moments, then her mouth curled up in disgust. 'This is no use to me,' she chided the President, 'a chicken was stolen and a chicken must be replaced!'

'Fine,' said Mandela and returned to the neighbour. The ten rand was returned and after much haggling, the neighbour eventually relented and bought another live chicken. Pleased with the way things were turning out, the President went back to the woman and presented her with the bird. She stared at it for a few moments and then sniffed dismally, saying, 'It is a pitiful bird and nowhere near as fat as mine was. It simply won't do.'

'Fine,' said Mandela and returned to the neighbour yet again, and again after even more intense bargaining, he finally managed to elicit yet another fowl from him. Once again he presented his spoils to the woman. Finally this time he'd done it right and was rewarded with a smile. Two chickens were indeed just exchange for the loss of her one fat bird! She would feast on one that night and return the second bird to her yard to fatten up and hopefully lay some eggs. Everything had turned out for the best and out of a bad situation her fortunes had in fact vastly improved, she told Madiba. And that night Mandela was the toast of the entire community – as they drank traditional African beer in praise of the great success of his negotiating skills.

If only the conflicts elsewhere in Africa were that simple!

PRISON AUSTERITY COMES TO QUNU

There is also no doubt that Mandela's humble manner is genuine and not simply put on as a political ploy. Mvezo was the place of his birth, the place that had instilled into the young Mandela his political beliefs, his love of the land and his noble bearing – values that were to play a great part in his destiny and beliefs that would stand him in great stead throughout both his long years in prison and his five-year tenure as President. He often said in public that he 'knows every rock, every blade of grass and all the cattle' in the small rural village of Qunu, his home, very near to Mvezo. It's almost as if he is only ever truly at peace in Qunu.

Ironically, the first house he built in Qunu was not reflective of the normal structures of the area. It was in fact a reminder of another period in his life, namely his incarceration of 27 years in South Africa's prisons. The house is very simple, almost austere – a carbon copy of his last 'prison cell', the warder's cottage at Victor Verster Prison in the Western Cape. It was there that he spent his last years behind bars. But by his own account, it was one of his busiest times as he was locked in secret negotiations with the South African government of the day. It was also one of his happiest times – a time he could spend reading, studying, thinking and preparing for his eventual release from jail. And little did he know then that these were all activities he would have very little time for after his release, due to his hectic schedule. In fact he often jokes that he misses prison and all the free time he had in which he could do exactly as he pleased.

With these amazingly happy memories in mind, the house in Qunu was built as a standard, regulation government structure. It was constructed to exactly the same specifications as his Victor Verster 'jail'. A truly remarkable request when one thinks about it. Here was a man who had stayed in the most luxurious of palaces, the most opulent of guesthouses and the world's finest hotels. A man who had been fêted by kings and queens, presidents and prime ministers and yet he was most comfortable in this simple abode. Unlike some of his counterparts in the rest of Africa, who spent lavish fortunes on presidential residences while the rest of the country starved, Mandela just didn't need any of it. He spent little more than a handful of nights at the massive presidential residence in Pretoria, and never bothered to refurbish it to his taste. He far preferred returning home to his more simple home in Houghton in Johannesburg, despite the fact that it meant a good 45-minute trip (and a little inconvenience to his bodyguards) to do so. And even when he and Graça bought a new home together in the same suburb, it was not over the top. Beautiful and exquisitely decorated (Graça Machel has impeccable taste), but no more extensive than the average home in the area.

The couple have since built a second house at Qunu, the first being earmarked for Madiba's son Mandla, the "farm manager".

AFRICANISING THE PRESIDENTIAL BODYGUARDS

The humble world of Qunu was something that the bodyguards also had to get used to. The first time Steyn visited the area he got a taste of the kind of lifestyle common to the area – certainly a far cry from the international trips he was used to accompanying the President on. Mandela had to attend the wedding of one of the sons of a local chief. The presidential party arrived by helicopter to find the chief a little drunk. And this at ten in the morning! Completely unimpressed, Mandela stepped out of his role as President and into his position as a senior member of the royal clan. He proceeded to give them a lengthy lecture in Xhosa when asked to 'say a few words' at the reception. He laid down the law, ordering them to sober up immediately and insisting that this kind of drunken behaviour had absolutely no place in Xhosa culture.

Like the rest of Mandela's life, his time in Qunu inspired several stories that became legend among the Presidential Protection Unit members. Whenever he went to the village he would take long walks, sometimes as long as six hours. On one particularly hot December day Mandela took one of his six-hour walks, really pushing it up and down the beautiful, rolling hills of the region. Bear in mind that we're talking about a man who was already just a few years short of 80. But it was the bodyguards who were taking the strain. They were growing increasingly dehydrated on this walk and radioed their colleagues to bring some water both for them and the President, working on the simple assumption that if they were thirsty, so was he. Not far behind this small party was a second team of protectors who had drawn the long straw and ended up driving one of the police 4×4 bakkies. It was inside this vehicle that the cold water was placed and quickly they caught up with the President and his tired team, offering to soothe their dry throats with ice-cold water. Well, instead of praise, the protection team received a heavy tongue-lashing. Mandela was not impressed when he saw the vehicle. 'Who told you to follow me?' he demanded. 'Who told you to bring me water? You are just wasting petrol! And oil! These people here don't know bakkies, they only know horses. Take this bakkie back to the house immediately!' *The practice of following out of range of sight in a vehicle is in fact a very sound security practice, and one that the PPU always followed, whether Madiba was walking in Cape Town, Houghton or Qunu. The bakkie was there not only to provide water, but also to offer mechanical assistance should something go wrong on the walk. Needless to say this taught us to be a lot more discreet.*

Another famous story is that of the sheep. Not only did the bodyguards have to develop a taste for the country, but their duties there were very different from those they had become accustomed to in the sophisticated city life of Johannesburg and the rest of the world. Based at Mandela's Qunu house was a family clan member who was really some sort of tribal household manager. His name was Nqoma. The King of the Pondos was coming to visit Mandela that week, so he called Nqoma and instructed him to go and purchase a sheep as a gift for the King. Nqoma duly did this, but later that evening Steyn received a telephone call from the President. He had an unusual request: "Rory, could you send two of the protectors with the 4×4 early tomorrow morning to go and buy another sheep as the one that

Nqoma had bought was 'quite pitiful'." Off they went with money provided by the President and bought the fattest sheep they could find, fit indeed for a King. Certainly there was nothing in the books about this sort of thing when they were undergoing their presidential protection training!

Another typical Transkei illustration was the mode of transport for the sheep back to the King's palace: legs tied together, in the boot of the King's Mercedes!

Animals are slaughtered in the traditional African way in the Transkei. That means no abattoirs or butcheries are involved. (Even if they wanted to use more pristine ways of killing a beast, none exist in the Transkei.) This is the rural heartland we are talking about, where animals are caught, slaughtered and cooked. This was a bit of a shock at first to the white city boys protecting Mandela, who were used to purchasing their meat cleaned and neatly packaged at their local supermarkets. Certainly there was no bone, gristle and hair to be removed. But they quickly learnt not only how to slaughter an animal, but also the tradition surrounding eating it. There is a strict hierarchy as to who eats meat and even what meat. For example, elder men get first choice of the best cuts and all the traditional African delicacies that go with this such as the liver, tongue and brawn. Children are very lucky to get anywhere near these things. But Madiba, because of his age and not his status, is one of the privileged few who gets his share of the very best. *Among his favourite foods are liver, sheep's tongue and brawn. He also loves* mphokoqo *(maize meal porridge with sour milk). And although it is difficult to eat meat in the traditional way at his Houghton home, he certainly makes sure he has* mphokoqo *for breakfast every morning. He likes his milk very sour and always says 'you must be able to smell it at a distance'.*

If it wasn't sheep it was bees. Steyn was seeing Mandela to the door of his Qunu house when the President remarked, 'Oh, these chaps are still here?' Steyn had no idea what Mandela was talking about but noticed that he was pointing towards some bees buzzing around a flower bed.

I asked him, 'Tata, what do you mean?'

'Didn't I tell you?' smiled the President. Seeing the confusion on Steyn's face, he proceeded to explain that the flower bed they were standing next to was just outside his bathroom window. The previous day, about seven or eight bees had flown in there and had stung him on his stomach and thighs while he was drying off after a bath. He thought that perhaps they'd been attracted by the smell of the bath foam. *I was immediately concerned, and asked him if he was sure he was okay. Quite nonchalantly, he brushed off the whole incident with a laugh, saying of course he was absolutely fine. He was, he reminded me, after all a country boy and quite used to this, having been stung many times before. It was no big deal.*

It was not long after this that Mandela's office, as well as Steyn himself, started getting calls from media organisations around the country inquiring after the President's health. There was even a rumour that he'd been rushed to hospital after being stung by a swarm of bees. *I was very angry at this irresponsible reporting and rushed to tell the President. I couldn't understand where this information had come from in the first place, as Qunu is pretty far from 'civilisation'. Imagine my surprise when the President told me with a smile that he, in fact, had planted the information among the press. He'd mentioned it tongue-in-cheek to a journalist over the phone that morning and was quite unperturbed that the information had leaked out.*

In addition to traditions surrounding food and the slaughtering of animals, Mandela took great pride in showing his bodyguards all the other places he spent time in during his childhood. He would show the huge iron pots that are used for cooking, the school where he first learnt to read and write, the ancient trees elders used to sit under as they wisely made decisions about the community. And on one occasion Mandela even cheekily showed a crowd of journalists and bodyguards the place where he first told a young girl that he loved her. However, he laughingly refused to give her name, as she was long since married to someone else and a respected member of the community. 'Her husband would not be impressed,' he said with a twinkle in his eye.

MIST, COWS AND OTHER RURAL HAZARDS

Another peculiar facet of the trips to Qunu was the weather. There was often a thick mist that descended over these mountain villages. *I have travelled the 30 or so kilometres between Qunu and Umtata more times than I care to remember. The mist on this particular part of the road can be as thick as pea soup, and yet very few drivers even bother to switch on their headlights. Many vehicles are not roadworthy and this area has one of the highest incidence of road deaths in the country. You risk your life every time you drive between the Holiday Inn in Umtata (where the bodyguards would stay) and Qunu.* The mist often also makes it extremely dangerous to land an aircraft in Umtata and there has been many an occasion when the presidential jet has been diverted to East London. The protection team would then have a two-hour drive to East London and another two hours back to Qunu through the same thick mist that prevented them from landing in the area in the first place. Not pleasant!

There were also other hazards at the small Transkei airport besides abysmal weather conditions. Before the small airport was fenced off, the job of a protector involved everything from ensuring the airport was open for business and the tower manned, to chasing roaming sheep and cattle that had wandered onto the area off the landing strip. And on one occasion the presidential plane could not land because the local authorities had decided on the spur of the moment to re-tar the landing strip – without telling anyone. The plane was duly diverted to East London. Now, not only was Mandela agitated at having to delay his arrival, but many of the bodyguards were keen to get to Qunu as quickly as possible, as there was a rugby test match against our arch-enemy – the All Blacks – that they wanted to watch during their free time. Instead the entire party was confined to the VIP lounge at East London airport. Now the work of the bodyguards really began. First up was to make the President a cup of tea. And that gave rise to their first challenge. Mandela drinks honey not sugar in his tea and there was nothing like this at this small-town airport. But ever the sport, the President gallantly agreed to have sugar. The second and far more serious problem facing the body-guards was finding a helicopter to transport the President to Qunu. All the plans had been thrown out of the window due to the landing problem. The only people with a helicopter were of course the South African Air Force. But here they ran into a huge problem: the rugby! Despite phoning everywhere they could not get hold of anyone. Eventually as night drew closer they managed to rouse an officer who could assist them. It turned out that everyone else who could have assisted the President was glued to the television sets watching the rugby match. When the presidential party eventually arrived in Qunu, it was dark and the President was somewhat irritated at having been delayed. But such is life in a rural area. The bodyguards quickly learnt to expect the unexpected and to develop creative ways of dealing with somewhat unusual problems.

On another occasion Mandela was visiting a different part of the country – Pietersburg, which is almost as rural as Qunu. The advance team had arrived ahead of the President, as was their custom and had the presidential BMW waiting for him. The cars had been washed and parked ready to whisk Mandela away the minute his plane landed. Bodyguard and driver of the President's vehicle that day, Johan Scott, was satisfied that everything was under control and settled down to relax before his boss arrived. He opened the car boot to retrieve his jacket in which lay a packet of cigarettes. But he was to commit one fatal error. He needed both hands to put on the jacket and to do this he put the keys down in the boot. Bad move – as anyone who's ever done this knows only too well. The next minute he pressed the boot closed with the car keys inside and, inexplicably, the central-locking system just clicked into place and the boot would not re-open!

The spare keys were miles away in Pretoria and the option of entering the boot via the rear seats was non-existent because of the steel armour-plating. There was still plenty of time before the presidential plane touched down, but given that they were miles away from 'civilisation' it was not going to be easy to get assistance. Scotty frantically phoned the BMW agent in Pietersburg and told them to get there as soon as possible. Well he spent a nail-biting hour waiting for their arrival but eventually, with just 20 minutes to go, he realised he would have to come up with another plan. Starting to sweat now, he decided to phone a locksmith and miraculously the man arrived just five minutes before the plane landed and managed to save the day as the Falcon was on final approach. He jumped into the driver's seat and locked and unlocked the doors manually and 'hey, presto!' the central locking unlocked the boot!

'Sweating? Sweating is not the word!' says Scotty.

These were both man-made near disasters, but on one occasion it was a natural disaster that threatened the President's life. The story made headlines around the country and was written up in the *Sunday Times* under the tongue-in-cheek heading 'Soap bars land Mandela in hot water'. But at the time it was not a joke, and ironically it was this natural disaster rather than an assassin's gun that was to pose the biggest threat to the President throughout his entire term of office.

It was nearing Christmas in 1998 and as usual Mandela was resting at his Qunu village. On this particular day he had asked his bodyguards to take him down to Umtata to a local pharmacy where he wanted to buy his favourite soap – a simple action that nearly cost the President his life. The weather patterns around the country had been particularly strange in the previous week with tornadoes and floods lashing some of the more far-flung regions. However, there was no way the protection unit could have predicted what was going to happen on this particular day. The soap was particularly important to Mandela as it was one he had favoured during his prison years and was not readily available in the cities.

Pharmacy floor manager, Stella Hawkes, said that Mandela usually asked her to tend to his needs when he visited the chemist. He had told her he had a dry skin condition and had asked for a specific soap.

'I showed him other health soaps . . . but the President, who knows his soap well, wanted the brand name *Sebamed*.

'This was the soap he had used in prison. It costs about 25 rand a bar and is non-allergenic and good for dry, sensitive skin,' she said.

'The President is very particular and he placed an order for a dozen bars of Sebamed.' While all this was going on, some of the bodyguards outside the chemist noticed a dark black cloud heading their way. But tornadoes and the like are not exactly common in South Africa, so they just dismissed it as bad weather as it was drizzling and windy anyway. They were used to storms and mist in the Transkei – nevertheless they looked at their watches and hoped the President would finish soon, as driving in the area's notoriously bad weather was not a pleasant experience. 'The next minute, while I was examining a bar, there was the shattering sound of glass. In panic, I threw the soap onto the floor and ran to the rear of the pharmacy,' Hawkes said. The bodyguards were also given little time to think and simply reacted instinctively. This was one of those moments when everything their training had prepared them for just kicked into gear. Afterwards, several of them commented that their first thought had been that it was a bomb that had gone off because all they heard was a massive explosion. It was an explosion all right, but not a man-made one. A giant, furious tornado had ripped through the small Transkei town of Umtata, shattering in an instant the large glass window of the chemist. Wreaking havoc in its wake, the tornado was so severe that 18 people were killed, more than 160 injured and hundreds left homeless as the massive tornado blasted its way through the town. It did all this damage in just ten minutes, but it was ten minutes that could have ended the President's life there and then. Speaking afterwards from his home in Qunu, which was just on the outskirts of the devastated town, Mandela told journalists, 'As I was in the chemist, I heard loud noises. The entire front window of the pharmacy caved in. My men pushed me down on the floor and then crouched over me, covering me with their bodies.

'It happened so quickly that I did not have time to think. My men reacted marvellously.'

What had actually happened was that as soon as the "explosion" occurred the men threw themselves onto Mandela, caring little for their own safety, but knowing instinctively that they had to protect the President.

'Would you take a bullet or risk your life for the President?' is a question his men and women are frequently asked. It's not something protection officers like talking about, and is certainly a moment most bodyguards hope they will never have to experience; and although they all, without exception, say they are willing to lay down their lives for Mandela, it's only when faced with an actual experience that one sees how people react. And in this case the bodyguards came through with flying colours. 'The whole scene reminded me of a television programme. My men completely ignored the danger to themselves and were solely occupied with protecting their President,' praised Mandela afterwards. 'If they had been killed, I would have been dragged out alive from underneath their corpses.'

The bodyguards' behaviour is all the more exemplary in that most of them, as mentioned earlier, believed it was even more serious than a tornado. The Cape Town team leader of the Presidential Protection Unit, Superintendent Thobile Mtwazi, said that when he heard the sound of breaking glass he thought it was a bomb blast.

'The President was next to a shelf looking at the soap while one of the people assisting him was working at a computer terminal. The guards reacted instinctively, pushing the President to the floor.

'Five of us got around the President and we crouched low over him. At that moment our lives were secondary. We were concerned only about guarding Madiba.

'We would gladly have died for him,' Mtwazi said. 'President Mandela must have been on the floor for about 15 minutes before we moved him to one of the consulting rooms in the pharmacy. We left him there with four men while we cleared a way out of the pharmacy.

'We were forced to drive on an island in the road to get away because it had been blocked by traffic and crowds of people. We then parked near the town's central police station, away from trees, and waited for about 15 minutes for the storm to subside before driving the President to Qunu.'

The President escaped without a scratch but two of his men were not so lucky.

Superintendent Michael Kupiso and Captain Jerome Hardenberg had to receive stitches for injuries to a foot and arm respectively after being cut by flying glass. Hardenberg agrees though that it was a privilege to protect the President. 'It didn't bother me and I did not feel any pain during the actual incident. It is our job to protect the President and I am privileged to do so.'

A little tornado was not going to stop the President from buying his favourite health soap, though. His guards returned to the shop that same day and managed to retrieve three bars from the debris. Then Mandela returned the next day during a presidential tour of the devastated area and a visit to those who'd lost loved ones. He also paid a courtesy call to the chemist, who made sure he was given another nine bars.

So a lucky escape for the President, but it turned out to be a crucial moment for his bodyguards, who received only praise and admiration from their superiors and their boss. Presidential Protection Unit Head Jason Tshabalala, speaking on Radio 702 afterwards, said, 'They are trained for many things but natural causes is another case altogether. But I must congratulate my colleagues whose quick thinking meant they could take control of the situation at the time. It was so quick; they just threw the President on the ground. His life was in danger and you don't negotiate when his life is threatened.'

And in the end, although it was a tough call, it turned out to be a situation in which they were able to prove that their protection skills ranked up there with the best of them. *That's something we've always known though!*

"...

A true story as told by
Nelson Mandela

One day I phoned to speak to somebody and a lady answered the phone. I asked to whom I was speaking. Instead of answering, she shouted, 'What is your name?' I said, 'No, I asked you first, to whom am I speaking?' We argued a bit, you first, me first, then she became angry and said, 'You sound like a very backward person. Have you got a matric?' I answered, 'Well, Madam, if the qualification to speak to you is the possession of a matriculation certificate, I will have to go and work very hard to obtain one so that I can be in your class.' 'You'll never be in my class!' she retorted, and banged down the phone.

..."

Section II

With Madiba on the campaign trail, Chatsworth, KwaZulu-Natal local government elections, June 1996.

Adil Bradlow

Madiba walking with Prince Charles from the Brixton Community Centre, London, July 1996. Stan Downey is immediately behind me (front left), Ashwyn Govind behind Madiba, with David Luddington (above) and Keith Low (below) on the right.

A clandestine photo of Madiba outside the Houses of Parliament, Westminster, 1961 or 1962, before his arrest.

Madiba outside the Houses of Parliament again, July 1996.

Peter Lynch

'Watch the hands' – Madiba greeting adoring school children outside Buckingham Palace, July 1996, with Ashwyn Govind in the No. 1 position.

With Naomi Campbell at Luthuli House, 1996.

With Madiba, Gill, Kyle and (as yet unborn) Iain at a lunch hosted by the President for his protection teams' families, Mahlamba Ndlopfu, August 1996.

The Leadership – Myself (team leader), Madiba, Sam Shitlabane (team leader) and Jason Tshabalala (National Commander), Mahlamba Ndlopfu, August 1996.

Cape Town Station – The launch of the Blue Train, Madiba and
Graça with (above) Mia Farrow, and (below) Archbishop
Desmond Tutu, September 1997.

The view from the front of the bus on the trip from Ras-Ajdir to Tripoli, Libya, October 1997.

At the back of the bus, with the Libyan ambassador to South Africa, Al-Zubeidi (middle), and the Libyan Prime Minister (left), October 1997.

Dr Dirk de Lange

Madiba and Colonel Muammar al-Gadaffi – State arrival ceremony, Tripoli, October 1997.

The monument erected outside the house in Tripoli that was bombed by US fighter aircraft, in 1985.

Dr Dirk de Lange

Rubbing shoulders
with Gadaffi.

Madiba with Gadaffi; the
latter wearing the Order
of Good Hope, Class I,
Gold, Zwara, Libya,
October 1997.

Madiba arriving in Edinburgh for the Commonwealth Heads of Government Meeting in Scotland from Libya, November 1997.

Nelson Mandela
CHILDREN'S FUND

The stunning front cover of the Nelson Mandela Children's Fund Annual Report, 1988, showing the blind boy 'seeing' Madiba with his hands.

THE THIRD YEAR

1998 ANNUAL REPORT

With the team – Des van Rooyen, Piet Irvia, Sean Dippenaar, Poti, Mike Maponya, Percy and Joe Chakale: Royal Swazi Sun, 1998.

With Zelda le Grange on board the *Falcon* – 'You have 73 voice messages!' This photo typifies the hectic schedule behind the scenes.

The official photo of the presidential couple – Houghton, October 1998, with Poti partially obscured.

Madiba saluting the crowd, with Mandla Moya (left of Madiba) and Selby Masikane (left behind Madiba).

Encouragement to let go! – Eldorado Park, 1999 Election trail.

Eldorado Park again – with Popi Lukhele (left), Election '99.

Keeping a watchful eye – Eldorado Park again, with Dennis Matlabe (left) and Johan Scott (foreground, right) Election '99.

The changing of the guard – the old and the new presidents –
Orlando Stadium, Election '99, with Chris Ngcobo (left) and Poti.
And that 'salute'!

My boys with Hansie's boys – at a lunch hosted by the President
at Mahlamba Ndlopfu on the eve of their departure to the Cricket
World Cup, May 1999.

Madiba and Shenge
(IFP leader Dr
Mangosuthu Buthelezi).
Madiba shows his gift
to the crowd, KwaZulu-
Natal, February 1999.

Rajesh Jantilal

Taking the opportunity
to convey a message to
'sceptical Siphiwe'
during a dance item in
Durban, April 1997.

Rajesh Jantilal

'Rory, have you arranged for me to greet the Police?', with Zulu King Goodwill Zwelithini, Durban 1997.

Alf Khumalo

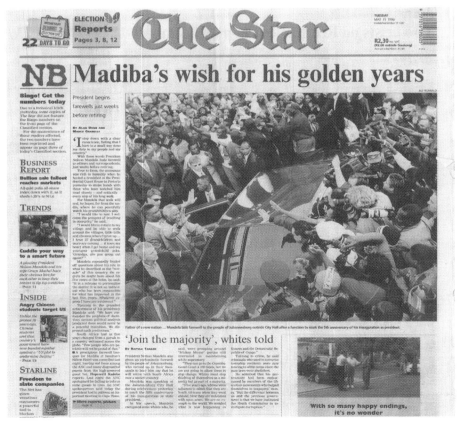

Rajesh Jantilal

This image captures the chaos we were sometimes confronted with. (Outside Johannesburg City Hall during the city's farewell to Madiba, May 1999.)

6

Behind the Legend

A president should wear a dark suit, a white shirt, a tie and a hat. My uncle dresses like a drunkard.
(Nelson Mandela's nephew commenting on his uncle's simple style of dress.)

Nelson Mandela may be an international icon. And he is certainly a legend in his lifetime, often far exceeding the myth that became Mandela while he was in prison. But behind this legend is a man of great simplicity, content with the smaller things in life. Unlike many leaders, he does not need the trappings of wealth and fame to make him happy. This simplicity comes across in everything he does – from the way he deals with people to his choice of toiletries.

A MAN OF SIMPLICITY

Perhaps toiletries, then, is a good way to begin this chapter.

We were never briefed about this. But there are a number of things that are unspoken laws among the bodyguards. One of the first things you learnt was that you always had to know where Madiba's toilet bag and glasses were. Mandela did not by any means have extravagant tastes, but he was very particular about what products he used. And it was this particularity that caused many a problem for his eager-to-please staff.

This included old-fashioned razor blades wrapped in wax paper and an ancient brand of hair tonic. Often the bodyguards would be sent to the local pharmacy in search for these items. The first problem was the razor blades. Companies simply stopped making them and Mandela was forced to go for the modern variety. *One day he called me and said, 'Rory, come and show me how to use these.' He had a new Gillette Sensor razor. It was a simple clip-in razor that didn't need any fiddling, but to the President it was something he'd never experienced before, having spent so long in jail.*

Another problem was encountered with the hair tonic. The company had simply stopped making this specific brand. *In the last months of his presidency the paramedics assigned to my team had bought all the remaining boxes of the stuff. It came down to a situation where they literally only had three bottles left in the whole country! This I was told by the production manager of the company.* And so the President was finally forced to find another brand he could live with.

Even the medication he used for an infected throat bordered on the quaint. The modern method of treating an infected throat is to use a spray with a long nozzle. In Mandela's youth, it was a little brush attached to a bottle of medicine. *You would actually paint the medication onto your throat. When I asked the pharmacist for this, he laughed and said it went out years ago.* Such was the legacy of 27 years behind bars.

But more than a prison legacy, Mandela was also a product of his generation. His bodyguards would attest to the fact that although he was not vain, he was very particular. *If you didn't know where his toilet bag was, you were in trouble.*

He would also not go out in public without his shoes being polished. *The President would often call me after a rally and ask, 'Rory, do you mind just dusting my shoes off?' And when we flew in a helicopter he would always wear a radio-headset exactly the same as that worn by the pilots. We would always keep the door shut after landing so that he could comb his hair neatly. I guess this is all part of the generation he comes from. You just don't go out in public look-ing ungroomed. I admire that in him. He's a real gentleman.*

Not only is Mandela a gentleman, but much has been written about him being something of a ladies' man in his youth; a man who had a fine appreciation of good clothes and was always seen sporting the very latest, snappiest gear. And upon his release from prison, Mandela certainly kept his image as one of South Africa's best dressed men, enhanced by his own particular style in the form of his 'Madiba shirts'. Many people lay claim to introducing Mandela to these shirts. A woman in Cape Town once presented him with five of the shirts and there is one theory that he liked them so much, he simply continued to have them made. Another story states that he was shopping in Thailand when he saw these beautiful silk shirts. He bought several of them to take back to South Africa. And since then, Johannesburg draper Yusuf Surtee has been importing them for the President. Whatever the real story is, they have certainly become Mandela's fashion signature. And the shirts were responsible for one of his more famous quips: Archbishop Tutu once bemoaned in public the fact that Mandela dressed too casually and didn't wear suits often enough. Mandela laughingly dismissed these complaints, saying, 'And this from a man who wears a dress!'

Such was his penchant for stylish dressing that he even caught the eye of the French *Elle* magazine, which wrote a lengthy feature on the President – complete with him modelling his own taste in clothing. As he grew into his presidency, Mandela became more and more famous for wearing his Madiba shirts. He was not fond of suits and only really wore them for ceremonial occasions. Eventually, protocol officers became used to his stubborn disregard for pompous apparel. And far from being sloppy, his beautiful silk shirts spawned a fashion industry dubbed 'Madiba chic'. He would wear these everywhere, from banquets with the Queen of England to local community jaunts. Another one of Madiba's favourite stories illustrates this. A prominent nephew of his was once publicly asked what he thought about his uncle's dress sense. He replied, 'A president should wear a dark suit, a white shirt, a tie and a hat. My uncle dresses like a drunkard!'

Protocol should have realised very early on what was in store for them. The most famous incident involving Mandela's dislike of formality happened right at the very beginning of his presidency. He was sitting in his lounge discussing with his two aides, Jessie Duarte and Barbara Masekela, what he was going to wear to his inauguration in May 1994. Mandela did not even want to wear a suit, arguing that it would remove him from the people. But they insisted, saying he looked so handsome and that it was appropriate for the occasion. In fact, they went so far as to press for a tuxedo complete with bow-tie. But Mandela wasn't having any of it. 'It makes me feel like a penguin,' was his retort. In the end they prevailed upon him to wear a suit. But once he'd assumed power, he felt more free to develop his own dress style and to choose the clothes he wore.

The Presidential Protection Unit soon learnt to adapt to Mandela's stylish dress code. The only time they would dress informally was at a political rally or if they were collecting the President in the middle of the night when no one was around to see them. In those cases it could be jeans and tackies. But other than that, it was a suit and tie or blazer and tie. No lumber or leather jackets for them. For ceremonial occasions, the team leader would put out the word that members had to wear a dark suit.

The simplicity displayed by his taste in clothes and his often old-fashioned values touched many other parts of Mandela's life. He received a vast number of gifts during his term of office. Most of them went into a safe and have now been placed in the museum in Umtata. Some of the gifts have been presented to him personally and not in his capacity as head of state. *And he appreciates them all from the most simple to the more extravagant. He gets really annoyed if his over-boisterous grandchildren break anything, or if staff members misplace or lose his gifts.*

Perhaps even greater than his simplicity is Mandela's complete lack of airs and graces. One simply cannot imagine Mandela going the way of some African heads of state who revel in tasteless luxury and opulence.

Certainly his travels have taken Mandela everywhere, and, being an ordinary human being, he obviously often needs to go to the toilet whether it is in a remote rural area or the most lavish of accommodations. *One of the standard duties of the advance protection team is to find and assign a toilet to the President. When we asked organisers about it, they would often say, 'No, the President can't use that loo.' But he just doesn't mind. He will use anything available, from the most rudimentary corrugated iron long drops or trees and bushes, to state-of-the-art palatial cloakrooms.* And from toilets to beds, no matter where in the world Mandela finds himself, from London's Dorchester Hotel to the White House, he will always make his own bed.

The same goes for Mandela's pens. His standard choice is an ordinary Bic Fineliner. After all, a writing implement is just that and anything will do. So one would see him at some lavish occasion pulling out his simple Bic Fineliner to sign an important official document, while his counterpart would brandish the very latest and most expensive designer pen. *I use a Parker Sonnet fountain pen and one day I had to surrender it at an official signing ceremony because the President didn't have a pen with him. Madiba enjoyed writing with it and asked me if he could continue using it for the rest of the day. This particular pen had sentimental value for me and so at the end of the day I asked for it back, but promised to purchase one for him if he liked it. I got Parker to send a collection of their finest pens and he chose two Sonnets similar to mine. But no amount of instruction succeeded in getting him to learn how to refill it and keep it operational. So after all that, it was back to the good old trusty Bic Fineliner. Although if Graça has anything to do with it, that won't last long either. She often feels obliged to remove the President's Bics from the top pocket of his 'Madiba shirt' whenever he has to appear in public or before the TV cameras!*

A comfortable briefcase was another Madiba trademark. Mandela probably has more briefcases than anyone could imagine. Most of them were gifts received during his travels abroad and many of them sport the finest luggage labels in the world. *But Madiba had one ordinary, worn briefcase, and during the five years of his presidency he changed it only once. And the only reason for this was because it was starting to look really tatty. He literally used things till they fell apart.*

From pens to briefcases and even to cars, Mandela never wavered in his preference for simplicity. Although he was extremely particular about the interior condition of his official vehicle, he never seemed to notice what particular make of car he was driven in. Cars were not status symbols for him. *A car to Madiba was simply a means of getting from A to B. Quite often he would see a guest off and then walk towards his waiting convoy attempting to get into the nearest car available. On several occasions I actually had to stop him from getting into one of the escort vehicles, usually a modest family sedan. They were just all the same to him and he hardly seemed to notice one make from another.*

THE QUEST FOR NORMALITY

Having spent so long in jail, it's perhaps understandable that Mandela wanted to be treated like an ordinary citizen. He wanted to be free to enjoy the simple pleasures of life. But being Mandela, it was obviously well near impossible. He tells a wonderful story in this regard. It was nearing Christmas and Mandela wanted to treat all the children in his family to chocolate. Now it's common knowledge that he has a large family, so he obviously has a lot of children to treat. Being Mandela he wanted to do it all himself, but it was late in the day and he didn't have much time. So he telephoned a chocolate manufacturer and asked for the number of the general manager. The woman who had answered the phone, not realising who was on the other end of the line, said she had no idea where the manager was or how to get hold of him. So he said fine, and phoned their competitor.

He managed to reach a senior employee who said he would keep the factory open for the President. Mandela had a large order – 12 boxes of chocolates. He arrived there and was duly presented with a mountain of chocolate which the chocolatier's bosses attempted to give him free of charge. But the President was indignant. 'I told them that this is a business deal, and if they don't let me pay, I'll take my business elsewhere.' So they were forced to let him pay, but afterwards the President commented, 'I suspected afterwards that they didn't charge me the correct price, but instead gave me a huge discount.'

No doubt Mandela could have anything his heart desired, but he would always insist on paying for it or otherwise suggest that wealthy businesses plough their money into one of his many projects of upliftment.

DELIGHT IN THE SMALLER THINGS OF LIFE
Mandela is a man of routine. Perhaps this arises from his time in prison and certainly is a result of his advanced years. He will always wake up early, a habit forced on him in prison and one that he is simply unable to shake off, and sit down to a simple breakfast. *Mphokoqo*, fruit and mineral water every morning. Twenty-seven years of prison routine has left its stamp on the President. The rest of his diet is also extremely simple and quite plain.

Until very recently Mandela would never touch such seemingly exotic items as prawns or champagne. But one should point out that since he's met Graça, like any man in love, food has taken on a new meaning. He relishes Mozambican prawns cooked with a healthy dose of peri-peri and will now often delight in a glass of sweet wine. But he won't touch chocolates or cakes – he simply doesn't have a sweet tooth. His main weakness is peaches, particularly the yellow cling variety. He's been known to eat so many peaches in one sitting that it earned him the fond nickname from Josina Machel, Graça's youngest daughter, of 'the peach-man'. Being such a popular president, Mandela of course was often given fine chocolates or fruit and nut arrangements as gifts, but he always passed these on to the children. 'He eats very healthily,' says his personal assistant, Zelda la Grange. 'Although he is fond of the occasional curry, his diet consists mainly of fish and other healthy items. You won't ever see him popping off for a greasy takeaway. Pizzas,

hamburgers and fried chicken are just not in his realm of experience.' On the subject of takeaway food, he has been known to
indulge in Nando's chicken. But only in very specific circumstances.

Mandela developed the habit of visiting the ANC's
Johannesburg Headquarters (known as Luthuli House after
Chief Albert Luthuli, South Africa's first winner of the Nobel
Prize for Peace) every Monday morning during his ANC presi-
dency. He only really stopped doing this when he stepped down
as ANC president at the end of 1997.

His personal assistant at Luthuli House, Beryl Baker, would
make sure that there was always a good supply of this chicken
whenever the President was in the building. But this led to a
very amusing incident on one occasion. The President was due
to attend a function and the organisers made the mistake of
inquiring after his eating tastes from Beryl, instead of going
through the official protocol channels. 'Oh, he always eats
Nando's,' was Beryl's unsuspecting response, not realising who
was asking and why. So that night at a glittering black-tie dinner,
the guests were all served with delicious fresh fish and prime
cuts of beef, while all Mandela had on his dinner plate was
Nando's chicken. The poor President was most disconcerted as
he gazed longingly at everyone else's plate piled high with fish or
fillet and wondered why he had been treated so differently.

Simple tastes in food also extended to simple ways of relaxing
in the little free time Mandela had during his presidency. One of
his greatest enjoyments was to be able to read, and during his
term of office he would constantly bemoan the fact that he
missed prison because it afforded him so much free time. But he
did at least insist on reading as many newspapers as possible
every day. When he was in Johannesburg he would read every
daily, that is *The Star, Beeld, Business Day, The Citizen* and *The
Sowetan.* On a weekly basis he ensured that he looked at the *Mail
& Guardian* on a Friday, *Saturday Star* and *Naweek Beeld* on
Saturdays and, of course, all the Sunday papers. *And when I say
read, I really mean it, because Madiba literally read a paper from*

cover to cover. Although the papers were delivered to him, his bodyguards learnt that if for some reason they were not there, they had to go and buy them.

They also knew that while the President was tolerant of most things, he didn't like the papers to have been read by others before they got to him. The bodyguards would also 'clean' the papers for the President, namely remove the classified sections, all the loose adverts, and often the entertainment segment as he was not particularly interested in this. His office would also make sure that he read magazines and other articles if they thought there was something of specific interest to the President. In the car, the President would listen where possible to local and national news stations. *There was many a time that the whole team stood deployed around the official vehicle, while the Old Man finished listening to the news. And every night he watched SABC news and more recently e.tv news as well. If he thought he was going to be home late, he made sure somebody in his household taped the relevant news bulletins for him.*

However, movies and other television programmes were simply not in his sphere of interest and he would rather spend his time reading a good book. All the fuss made about the *Titanic* made him enquire about this movie. Zelda bought the movie and he spent an interested three hours in front of the television with Josina.

A DISTRUST OF MODERN TECHNOLOGY

Part of his simplicity also stemmed from a distrust of anything modern – a characteristic often displayed by the elderly and even more pronounced in Mandela's case due to his long incarceration. He simply had no idea when it came to all the 'mod cons' of the late 20th century. The man who had the world fawning over him was unable to set a VCR to record a programme (a problem that he probably shared with many South Africans above a certain age!). He had to ask his grandson to record any television programmes he wished to watch.

And as for mobile phones, they were a complete mystery to him. He had a cell phone in his official vehicle but never carried it with him. He'd far rather pick up a land-line phone and telephone someone himself than get his secretary to do it. For a man of his age, he had a remarkable ability to remember telephone numbers and thought nothing of phoning anyone at any hour of the day. Many a person was been caught out by Mandela phoning them directly, and in disbelief simply hung up on the President thinking it was only another prankster among the plethora spawned by Mandela's unique accent.

South African cricketer Lance Klusener related in a television interview in London, after he had been named Man of the Series at the 1999 Cricket World Cup, that he had received a call from Mandela congratulating him on the achievement. Klusener said he immediately thought it was some radio presenter back home taking the mickey out of him. It so happens that Klusener speaks Zulu fluently (hence the nickname 'Zulu') and he decided there was only one way to ascertain whether it was really Mandela he was speaking to. He spoke to the caller in Zulu, and the President duly answered him in the same language. *Voila*!

The personal phone calls also extended to heads of state around the world. Mandela was probably one of the few presidents who could pick up a phone and be connected to anybody instantly. His personal assistant, Zelda la Grange, has one of the most prestigious telephone and address books around.

And if he was not phoning people personally, Mandela made sure he wrote everything down by hand. There was no thought of computers, dictaphones, let alone anything as sophisticated as e-mail and the Internet. Even the additional chapters on 'The Presidential Years' that will be incorporated into an updated edition of his book *Long Walk to Freedom*, have been handwritten.

Madiba also had very little regard for the value of money. He was not at all materialistic and money was simply there for a purpose. Sometimes he would ask his bodyguards to go and purchase hamburgers for his grandchildren and give them R10, thinking it was enough! At other times he would ask for a newspaper and hand over a R200 note. When he wanted something, he invariably looked at his coins first and on occasion even handed over American dollar bills which he kept in his wallet as well. But even if a bodyguard spent little more than R2 of his own money on something such as a newspaper for Mandela, he would always insist on paying that person back. He spent very little on himself. He was extremely generous with his money. He lavished presents on those he loved, donated generously to the charitable funds he himself set up and would constantly chide businessmen and women to give more financial assistance to those in need.

His grandchildren have certainly cottoned on to his generosity. On one occasion they were playing a virtual soccer game on a massive television screen. It's the kind of new-age computer game that little children adore but that doesn't come at all cheap. When asked who gave them their new toy, one of the grandchildren (who was no more than six at the time) responded, 'My grandfather.' When he was told how lucky he was to have such a generous grandfather, the child responded flippantly by saying, 'He must spoil us because he spent so long away from us in prison!'

Spending so much time in prison means Mandela has little regard for modern printing and publishing methods. *When he opened the Nelson Mandela museum in Umtata in February 2000, he was walking through reading some of the information signs at the various displays. He noticed a spelling mistake on one of them and to the amazement of the curator and others present, whipped out his Bic fineliner and corrected the mistake in his own hand!*

A LOVING GRANDFATHER

And spoiling his grandchildren is something Mandela is very fond of doing. If there is one thing Mandela regrets about his time in prison, and perhaps it is safe to say the only thing he regrets throughout that entire time, it is that he never got to be a real father to the two children he had with Winnie Madikizela-Mandela. But while he might feel that because of circumstances, that he has failed with his own children, he has certainly made up for it with his grandchildren.

Prior to his retirement, Mandela was fond of saying that he couldn't wait to end his term of office because then he would have time to read and play with his grandchildren. But in fact he'd been doing this in earnest long before he reached the age of retirement. Mandela takes his duties as grandfather extremely seriously and has actually taken over the responsibility for bringing up four of them. Mandla, Ndaba, Mbuso and Andile have been living in his Houghton home almost from the time he came out of jail. They are the sons of Makgatho, the son born out of his first marriage, to Evelyn. Very little is known of Makgatho. Being a private, family matter, the circumstances are not publicly known, but in true African tradition, the four boys moved in with their grandfather, the President.

Living with so many children is bound to keep anyone young, and particularly somebody with Mandela's boundless energy. He adores them; it's almost as if he's been given a chance to be a father to them. But he's also very strict and sets limits just like any good parent should.

Mandla, the eldest, first came to public attention at Mandela's eightieth birthday celebration. A tall, handsome young man, everyone had cause to comment on his remarkable likeness to his grandfather. But hearts were really set aflutter when Mandla gave a speech on behalf of the family to toast Mandela's birthday and, as it would happen, his marriage to Graça Machel. The speech was straight from the heart and brought tears to many an eye. And it was long remembered as one of the most charming things about that evening.

It's clear that Mandela is grooming Mandla for a place in public life. He's also been adamant that Mandla have a love for his rural heritage and he's been trained to take over the running of the Qunu household. Mandla has been made a farm manager but his interests also lie in far broader things. Right now he's studying for a degree in business economics and has a keen interest in politics as well as the fortunes of Africa's favourite soccer team, the *Amakhosi*. He has also developed the famous Mandela charm and is increasingly at ease in front of large groups of people. It will be interesting to watch his development over the years to come.

The other children are still a lot younger and need a strong father figure in their lives. While tackling his hectic schedule as president, Mandela made sure that he fulfilled this role. He was definitely more often the strict parent than the doting grandfather content to let them get away with murder. He was constantly berating them for their lack of tidiness and it was not strange for him to surprise them with a midnight patrol of the house. If he entered their bedrooms and found their rooms a mess, the lights would be switched on and the children woken up and immediately ordered to rectify the situation. But far more than cleanliness, one of the most important traits Mandela has tried to instil in the boys is a deep commitment to integrity and, above all, honesty. He does not tolerate lies and can be quite harsh in dealing with offenders.

Behind this strict disciplinarian is a heart of gold. Perhaps the best gift Madiba is giving these young boys is unconditional love. He adores them. He has a favourite ritual when he's been away from home. As he arrives the younger boys will scuttle behind the curtains on either side of the front door. Mandela will then pretend he hasn't noticed and address Graça; 'I wonder where Andile and Mbuso are. Can you see them? I can't see them anywhere. Where could they have gone?' And all this of course to nervous giggles and titters from behind the curtains until the children, bursting with eagerness, jump out and he pretends to be very surprised to see them! And although he is firm with them, he will be the first one to spoil the children.

On any given weekend, if you pop into Mandela's Houghton household, you will be greeted not by presidential pomp and show but the normal hubbub of suburban domesticity. Many times an important conversation with the President will be interrupted by Mandela telling the children to quieten down a little. This of course will last for a few minutes, before the noise begins again. And like any parent, Mandela has his moments of sheer concern for the children.

For example, when shortly before his marriage to Graça the household moved to a bigger and better house in the same neighbourhood, they also inherited an enormous swimming pool.

Madiba had a net put over it, and is not at all keen for the boys to play near the pool. But all such images of the President as grandfather only serve to add to his charm.

A FITNESS FANATIC

Walking was always Madiba's favourite form of exercise. It is only in recent years that he's been forced to cut down and has now stopped this form of exercise altogether, following problems with a troublesome knee. His bodyguards quickly became used to his routine. It would start early in the morning (on duty at 4:30 a.m.), with walks starting at 5:00 a.m., often being completed long before the sun came up. These walks would be followed by a heavy schedule of work during the day. Mandela's pace was so exhausting that he would often tire bodyguards three times younger than himself.

The President was fond of greeting people on his daily walks. Whether he was at his Gauteng home in Houghton or attending to business in Cape Town and staying at his residence there, Genadendal, it became something of a craze to try and spot the President on one of his regular walks. *This presented a unique challenge to the PPU and we quickly had to adapt our strategies to cope with it.* In Cape Town, Mandela would literally start walking off in any direction, deciding on the route as he went along. The bodyguards would accompany him the whole way, never quite sure where he was going. A car would be close by, not so much following as circling the block, but always in radio contact in case of an emergency. *It all presented a unique challenge to us as we had to adapt both our formation and our communication. To enable the pointsman and protectors in front of the President, who had no idea where he would go that particular day, to remain in their positions, the team leader would hurriedly communicate each new turn of the route to them.*

Mandela struck up several friendships along the various routes. There was a bread deliveryman who would only be starting his morning rounds as Mandela was passing. Then there were the usual Cape Town joggers, cyclists and walkers, who were often dumbfounded when Mandela stopped to greet them during their daily exercise.

One story that always comes to mind when talking about Madiba's walks is when we were in Cape Town for the opening of parliament in 1996. It was a drizzly February morning and we were once again walking along Main Road, Rondebosch. There was Troy Irving, Linga Monogamy, five or six Cape Town PPU members and myself. I was walking about five metres behind Madiba and due to a radio problem could not call Troy who was walking about 20 metres in front of him. In order to attract Troy's attention I picked up an acorn and threw it over Madiba's head at Troy. Having proved successful in getting his attention, I threw another two or three acorns at him out of fun or boredom. Something about this alerted Madiba however; either he heard them flying high over his head or he caught the movement of my arm in his peripheral vision. But he stopped and turned around with his hands on his hips and began to say something. However, by the time he'd turned around he saw me with an umbrella in one hand and a torch in the other! I had transferred the torch in my right hand to the left hand also holding the umbrella to throw and then back again, and it was milliseconds later that Madiba turned around. He must have had a moment's hesitation and decided to say nothing and continue walking. I felt like a kid with my hand in the cookie jar – but it was more like my heart in my mouth and, needless to say, that was the last time any acorns were thrown on those walks.

On the day of the opening of parliament in 1996, Mandela got up as usual for his early morning walk. He had completed about half of it; but as he was walking up a particularly steep hill past The Baxter Theatre, he began holding his kidneys – a sure sign that he was tired. The shortest way back was along De Waal Drive (one of Cape Town's busiest freeways). By now it was around 6:00 a.m. and starting towards peak-hour traffic. Here were the bodyguards with their torches on, waving traffic into the right-hand lane so that Mandela could walk freely and easily on the narrow pavement. Imagine the surprise of irritated motorists who peered out of their windows to see what the prob-

lem was, only to discover none other than the President cheer-
fully grinning and waving at them. Needless to say, Mandela
returned safely to Genadendal and was in good time for the
opening of parliament.

A STICKLER FOR PUNCTUALITY

Being on time for parliament was particularly important in
Mandela's case. He is an absolute stickler for punctuality. Many
African countries, and South Africa is no exception, have gained
a reputation for what's known as 'African time': a catch-all
phrase that serves as a humorous and sometimes not so humorous excuse for being late for anything from a critical meeting to
a special state banquet. Mandela would have none of this. At the
start of his term of office, very few people were punctual but
slowly he taught them, if through no other means than simply by
embarrassing them. Mandela would make sure he always arrived
on time and embarrassed cabinet ministers or ANC national
executive members would shuffle their way into their seats
under the stern disapproving glare of their president.

In one particular case Mandela was due to attend the unveil-
ing ceremony of the tombstone of the late Thomas Nkobi (the
former Treasurer-General of the ANC). It was an early Saturday
morning appointment to be attended by the most senior and powerful politicians in the land. Shortly before the presidential
convoy was due to depart from the Houghton residence, Steyn
received an urgent call from his counterpart, Jason Tshabalala,
who was already at the graveyard. His frantic colleague suggested
to Steyn that they shouldn't leave the residence because nobody
had yet arrived at the site and he was deeply concerned that the
President would be the only one there, something that Jason and
others who worked with Madiba were quite accustomed to.

When Steyn informed Mandela of this, the President's face
turned to stone. He was having none of this. Not only were we
going to be on time, said Mandela, but in fact he insisted that we
leave right away, several minutes earlier than scheduled.
Mandela arrived well before time and was greeted by only a

handful of other VIPs, including then Gauteng Premier Tokyo Sexwale, who had arrived minutes before the President. Humiliated ANC officials arrived later and to their horror found that the ceremonies were already underway. Suffice to say that those caught out by Mandela's punctuality seldom made the same mistake twice.

There was another embarrassing incident where Mandela was the first to arrive. Former trade unionist and now Gauteng Premier Mbhazima(Sam) Shilowa was due to get married. Madiba was invited and was the very first guest to arrive. The invitation said 4:00 p.m. and Mandela was there, punctual as usual, at 3:50 p.m. *The President sat and waited and waited. The next guest to arrive was Jay Naidoo, half an hour after Mandela, who was getting very impatient by this time. And eventually Shilowa, the bride and most of the guests showed up. But it was well after 5:00 p.m.*

GOOD NEIGHBOURLINESS

No description of Mandela would be complete without some kind of insight into the way he treats people. Not only did he adopt reconciliation as the political motto of his presidency, but he also practised it on a daily basis. In essence, it was much more than reconciliation. His respect and regard for his fellow human beings were not put on for the sake of political expediency, but were an integral part of his character. The way Mandela embraces everybody from the most lowly to the most important is ultimately the essence of the man. There are so many delightful examples of this.

Some of them had rather amusing consequences, like the time when Mandela first moved into his Houghton residence. The natural thing to do in South Africa's black townships in a case like this is for the new resident to make sure he introduces himself and greets all his new neighbours. In 1994, some Houghton residents weren't quite used to the idea of black people living in their lily-white suburb. This was also a time of increasing white fear about the rising crime rate in neighbourhoods.

As was customary, the bodyguards performed the advance missions. One Houghton resident, on seeing the black body-guards at the gate, slammed his security gate in their faces. Another resident saw the bodyguards' white minibus parked on the pavement outside his gate as he was returning home. Warning signals went off and he automatically assumed the occupants were hijackers. With a terrified look on his face he drove straight past his own house and around the block. When he saw that the minibus hadn't budged he telephoned the police. There were a lot of red faces when police officers arrived on the scene to arrest suspected hijackers only to find a charming President Mandela instead. But not all the greetings of the neighbours were as disastrous. One person was so delighted that Mandela had stopped by to say hello, she did what any good neighbour would and baked him a delicious chocolate cake.

Good neighbourliness and simple acts of human kindness also extended to the people employed by the President. When one of his Cape Town-based protection officers, Marcus Griebbelaar, became a father in 1996, Mandela had one of his staff buy a congratulatory bouquet. He then had the other PPU members drive him round to Griebbelaar's home so that he could hand the flowers to his wife in person. And to his own staff he demonstrated unfailing courtesy including arranging a party for the wives and children of all his bodyguards. *That small gesture and the sacrifice of his time made it so easy for us as protectors to be away from home for the many long hours that it often took. And our wives appreciated the gesture so much it would literally be months before they would complain about never seeing us. On that particular occasion the President posed for individual photographs with each one of the 30-odd families of his protectors. Of course those photos now occupy pride of place in all our homes.*

There were to be many gestures like this. One day in January 1998, Steyn and his team dropped Mandela at home around 5:00 p.m., only to receive a personal call from the President about four hours later. 'Rory, I'm so sorry to bother you but a very important person from the struggle is on his deathbed and I must go and see him but I don't want to do so without an escort.'

The following month, one of the old staff members from the presidential residence in Pretoria passed away. Again Mandela made time to go and personally convey his condolences to the family in Makapanstad.

And it wasn't just people well known to the President who were at the receiving end of these extraordinary acts of generosity. Whenever he had to go to hospital for a consultation, he made a point of randomly stopping to visit patients in the wards. On the subject of things medical, Mandela had a very good relationship with all of the many doctors and specialists who served him during his presidency. To show his appreciation of their work he would often invite them to state banquets. *This, despite the fact that he was not always a model patient, often not following their medical advice thoroughly, especially when called upon to rest.* But although he sometimes acted contrary to medical advice, he was never one to complain.

Once, after a particularly difficult knee operation, Mandela paid a brief visit to Luanda, the capital of Angola – a country where civil war has been raging unabated for over 20 years. And apart from the widespread devastation and loss of human life, the infrastructure of the place is virtually non-existent. This extends to the most basic of things, including hotel lifts.

In 1996 there was really only one decent hotel in Luanda and even that was simply not up to international standards. In such instances there is always a squabble between the protectors of the various heads of state over the use of lifts. There were only two small service lifts working in this hotel. *We were on the sixth floor and the meeting was on the ground floor. By the time we were ready to go down, these two solitary lifts had long since been commandeered by bodyguards higher up in the hotel. There was a choice between waiting and risking being very late for the meeting or walking down the stairs. There was not a moment's hesitation on the part of Madiba. Bad knee and all, he simply said, 'Let's walk.' And so against all medical advice, this 78-year-old leader walked down six flights of stairs along the hotel fire escape.*

Particularly close to the President's heart are children. As mentioned previously in this book, Mandela instituted the practice of inviting children to share his birthday in July of every year. There were huge parties focusing on different sectors of disadvantaged children from the homeless to the disabled to the abused. Christmas was also not reserved solely for himself and his family. This was a time when he went to rest at Qunu; but every year without fail there would always be a magical Christmas party, complete with presents and the perfect Santa Claus for the children of the village.

There were times during his presidency when Mandela received sharp criticism for caring only about black victims of crime and abuse. In August 1998, the daughter of assassinated South African Communist Party leader Chris Hani and two of her friends were brutally raped. Mandela was in Cape Town when it happened, but immediately on his return to Johannesburg he had his bodyguards drive him straight from the airport to visit the Hani family. But then, equally, he would care about white victims of suffering. As already mentioned, he flew to Secunda to a traditionally conservative white Afrikaner town for the sole purpose of visiting a terminally ill Afrikaner girl. When a child's dying wish is to meet Mandela, the President responds without a care for her skin colour.

STRONG-WILLED AND STUBBORN

The side the world usually sees of Mandela is the warm, charismatic man of the people. But coupled with this is a very strong will and at times downright stubbornness. It is these characteristics that defined his politics prior to his prison sentence. On a political level a strong will is essential in a leader, who will need it to stand up to the authorities where necessary and implement a vision even in the face of widespread disapproval. But on a personal level it can be tiring at times. And certainly the people most frequently at the receiving end of this stubbornness were of course his protection officers.

There were a few times, it would seem, when Mandela grew tired of being constantly surrounded by bodyguards. On one occasion right at the beginning of his presidency his security team had dropped him off at home, keen to end what had been an exhausting day. Already half the men were off duty, although, as was the practice, a group had remained on stand-by, should any need arise. But just after the convoy members had departed Mandela's Houghton residence, he suddenly changed his mind and decided he needed to go out again. PPU Head Jason Tshabalala's heart dropped. He'd sent most of his guys home and there was now only a skeleton team around the President, as the uniformed police stationed permanently at Mandela's home would now take over official responsibility for his security. But the only problem was that 'stationed permanently' meant exactly that: they could not move from their posts as their job was to guard the house even when the President wasn't there.

Mandela had informed Tshabalala that he wanted to go and visit Amina Cachalia. Recovering quickly, Tshabalala told the President that was no problem but he just had to go and recall the men on stand-by. However the President was impatient and had no desire to wait while they all came back. 'Her house is just around the corner,' said Mandela. He added, 'Look I really don't need you guys. And anyway Christmas only comes once a year. Can't you just overlook this just this once and give me an early Christmas present.' The President of course, besides being keen to get the visit under way, was taken with the novelty of going it alone for a short while. But Tshabalala was having none of it. He insisted on recalling his men. And instructed the stationary guards to make sure that Mandela did not leave the premises alone. A few minutes later, Tshabalala received a call from a very nervous guard informing him that the President was insisting that he leave NOW. And naturally this guard was too intimidated to argue. Tshabalala ordered him to keep the President there and rushed back outside. But he was too late; Mandela had already disappeared – off to Cachalia's house – on foot! When Tshabalala caught up with him, he apologised, but with a twinkle in his eye exclaimed just how much he'd enjoyed playing truant.

Playing truant was something the President had tried a few times at the very beginning of his presidency in 1994. Mandela moved into what is now the Presidential Guest House, next door to what is now Mahlamba Ndlopfu, his official residence in Pretoria. The bodyguards occupied some of the adjoining flats on the Bryntirion Estate and were a phone call away. Working on the premise that Madiba had the entire estate to walk around on (it is very big, housing ministers' homes and its own golf course, and is guarded around the clock by uniformed police) they were comfortable with giving him his space, especially on weekends. PPU protector Victor Solomons, who was in charge of security at the residence, tells how he received a frantic call from a gate guard one Sunday afternoon. Madiba had simply walked down to the main gate, greeted the policeman on duty and stepped out into Government Avenue and continued strolling. Solomons eventually caught up with him heading over the ridge on which Mahlamba Ndlopfu is located. This was when he did not yet enjoy the trust or support of Pretoria's white community, and in terms of his own security it was not a good move.

Naturally this kind of incident did not happen too often. But even once or twice was more than enough to give his protectors near heart attacks. A would-be assassin only needed one opportunity to strike. The above examples, however, occurred during the pre-1994 election campaign.

There was also the time that Madiba wanted to go to Luthuli House on an unscheduled visit. There were no bodyguards around who could drive him there as he was supposed to be resting. So what did Madiba do? He took a minibus taxi!

In another incident that gave his bodyguards an even worse scare, Mandela had been touring the country and his bodyguards had just spent three gruelling days co-ordinating his protection. With a much smaller team than would be assigned to him as head of state, these men were ensuring the advance work was properly done and keeping up with Mandela's demanding schedule. They finished their day's work in Nelspruit and finally VIP Protection Head Gary Kruser went to the the then ANC President and suggested that because the bodyguards were so tired and there was no replacement team, they leave a little later than usual for Mandela's traditional morning walk. Mandela, however, had other ideas. He was more than happy to allow his bodyguards to sleep in; in fact he was quite concerned about their health. His solution was that he would go for his walk on his own. Of course Kruser rejected that suggestion immediately and, resigning himself, said that the bodyguards would get up early as usual. The President disagreed and equally vociferously Kruser refused to capitulate. Eventually it was decided that the walk would not go ahead and the President went to bed. But Kruser was still a little suspicious and so just for good measure took the key of the hotel room away, locking Mandela inside. As usual, guards were posted outside his door and told to keep a vigilant watch on the room, at the same time ensuring that the President did not leave the place on his own.

Kruser woke at 5:30 a.m. and decided to pop down to Mandela and find out if he still wanted to go for a walk. To his horror, as he entered the room, he discovered that Mandela was not there. Furiously he turned to the men who'd been posted outside his room and demanded an explanation. They said they'd been there the entire time and had not moved the whole night. Rushing down to reception, Kruser asked the hotel manager if he'd seen Mandela. 'No,' was the response, but he had called earlier to say he'd lost his key and could they bring him a new one. He'd then let himself out and the bodyguards posted outside his door did not notice a thing as they were fast asleep. The team rushed outside and up the main highway in Nelspruit and there to their horror was Mandela weaving in and out of traffic as he went about his morning walk. 'It was such a relief,' says Kruser. 'What would I have told the country?' Mandela thought it was all rather amusing but he promised never to give them the slip again.

The practice of retaining the room key was to become one of Steyn's standard procedures whenever he was in charge of security when Mandela was travelling and staying in hotels, palaces or guest houses. *As long as the President had my telephone extension number in the room next door and I had the key under my pillow, I could sleep easy!*

AN ABILITY TO LAUGH AT HIMSELF

Stubborn he may be, but part of Mandela's charm is certainly his ability to laugh at himself. And a self-deprecating sense of humour is a seductive trait in anybody, let alone someone like Madiba. Over the course of his presidency, he developed the ability to deflect attention away from himself by making a joke out of the situation. One of these revolves around his best-selling autobiography, *Long Walk to Freedom.* The book has sold millions of copies around the world and been translated into many different languages. Mandela himself has personally signed thousands of copies of the book. On one occasion he was seen at the ANC headquarters surrounded by piles of books as he diligently signed each and every copy. The book itself is the definitive story of Mandela's time in prison and has won many an award both locally and internationally. But all this has, of course, not gone to his head. On the contrary, whenever Mandela sees people with a copy of the book who want it to be autographed, he will retort, 'Why are you reading such cheap literature?'

Another one of the lines he uses to make people feel less intimidated by him when they meet him is, 'I hope you still remember me?' Or if a person is so overcome with emotion that he is reluctant to come forward and shake his hand, Mandela will enquire, 'Yes, are you angry with me? You look angry.'

If he loses his place in a speech, Mandela will jokingly comment that 'You must forgive me and remember that you are listening to someone who is more than 80!' And he was renowned in parliament for poking fun at his advanced years. On his last day in the National Assembly, he even made fun in his final address of his impending retirement. He joked that now he was about to join the ranks of the unemployed and, with a new wife to provide for, people could expect to see him on the side of the road holding a cardboard placard reading, 'Unemployed, Large family to support, New wife!'

And even when he makes a mistake in a speech, Mandela will use the opportunity to gain a quick laugh. At the re-launch of the famous Blue Train, dubbed 'the finest train in the world', Mandela explained that he and Graça were travelling on its maiden journey because the train would be 'really good in help-ing to promote terrorism' (instead of tourism). Everyone fell about laughing and Mandela, quickly recovering, added that it was the fault of the chaps surrounding him that his thoughts had wandered to the subject of 'terrorists'. He was of course referring to people like Mac Maharaj (then Transport Minister) and other former Robben Island cell mates who were on the platform to welcome him and the First Lady. But not before both of them had had a good laugh at Madiba's *faux pas*.

SAINT AND SINNER

It goes without saying that even a man almost revered as a saint has his weaknesses. And Mandela will be the first one to admit this. He is not a saint – he is a human being who often makes mistakes just like the rest of us. Mandela will often say that he doesn't want roads, buildings, airports or hospitals named after him while he is still alive, as people don't know what will happen in the future. He believes he can only be finally judged on what kind of person he is after his death. This, nevertheless, has not prevented the plethora of public places, roads and insti-tutions, both in South Africa and abroad, that bear the Mandela name. And although Mandela finds the label of saint somewhat irritating, there are people who hold him in such high esteem that they do sometimes elevate him to that level. Grown men and women, on meeting him for the first time, have often been known to burst into tears. He is truly one of the most celebrated and instantly recognisable people in the world.

Throughout his presidency Mandela displayed an amazing

ability to reach out to people – and more often than not it wasn't just with words but with actions as well.

He donated a third of his salary to his Children's Fund and challenged business leaders to do the same. And in the latter part of his presidency he spent a huge amount of time travelling to the countryside and persuading businessmen and women to donate large sums of money to build schools and clinics in rural and poverty-stricken areas. But displaying just how smart he is, Mandela knows that very few people, if asked for a favour from him directly, will actually say no. So he took it upon himself to phone the wealthy personally and ask them to donate money to build a school, a hospital and so on. Their reward was that they got to travel to the area with the President and have the requisite photograph with him and generate a lot of publicity for their company.

Often Mandela would read in a newspaper of a hitherto unknown company that was doing particularly well. He would then instruct his assistant, Zelda, to find the number of its CEO. She would then often spend a whole day tracking down the business that hardly anyone had heard of. And then Mandela would phone and ask for their participation. After all, who was going to refuse the world's most popular and adored leader? *The Ekuseni Youth Centre was just one such example. Madiba opened seven schools and clinics in the former Venda, Gazankulu and Lebowa in 1996; and as this book was being written there were dozens of construction projects under way around South Africa, as Nelson Mandela answered the cry of his people. Perhaps it was the measure of the man, that when a young child asked for a school, the President responded. I don't think he'll ever stop either. He'll be working at this sort of thing until he draws his last breath.*

He is of course someone who displays genuine human weaknesses. He has made many mistakes, but his staff are so loyal that they have very little that is negative to say about him. The most one can find is that he is occasionally grumpy. This bad mood would usually be a result of his grandchildren behaving badly or, on a far more worldly note, when there is some kind of disaster in the country or if a member of his cabinet or parliament messed up in some way. His staff learnt to interpret his moods. Zelda la Grange says that she eventually knew just from the way that the President spoke to her what kind of mood he was in. 'If he was in a bad mood, he would phone and say "Zelda, please get so and so," and then just put the phone down. If he was in a good mood (which was particularly noticeable if he'd just spoken to Graça Machel), he would phone and say "Zelda, how are you? I am sorry to worry you again, would you mind phoning so and so." There would be a personal word or two and more often than not he would speak in Afrikaans.'

Zelda would often phone Steyn, who was the first in the morning to see the President, and ask what kind of mood he was in, especially if there was something sensitive she needed to discuss with him.

On the days the President was in a bad mood, his staff would find him distant and reserved. He would also get intensely caught up in the particular problem that was troubling him. For example, when violence had flared up in Richmond, he would phone anyone and everyone connected to it, at any time of the day. Says Zelda, 'It can be uncomfortable, but we learnt to deal with it and when the crisis was over, you would always be reassured that he was not angry with anyone in person, but rather intensely distracted by the problem.'

But as much as the President, like any person, could be grumpy or cross, he was extremely circumspect and would never, even in the presence of his closest staff members, say something bad about another person. 'He always seems to look at the best in a situation,' recalls Zelda. 'But he's also learnt over the years to be discreet and he will usually keep his thoughts to himself. Something which our younger generation should learn from him.'

A PRINCE AND A GENTLEMAN

Unfailingly polite, even when he is angry, Mandela is a true gentleman in every possible sense of the word. Perhaps it is his royal heritage or maybe he is simply a product of a generation that generally tends to be far more chivalrous. But either way, he is this curious mixture of African prince and Victorian gentleman. At times he will flirt outrageously with women and get away with it because he is so charming. If he were younger and not so famous, he'd probably be accused of being sexist. But although Mandela has often embraced the cause of women, he will still open a door for a lady, let her go first and never fail to compliment her on a special outfit. On one visit to Robben Island he offered to carry the bags and equipment of a female radio journalist, much to everyone else's amusement. And on another occasion, while attending talks with the Zulu monarch in Skukuza, he expressed concern that the huge crowd of waiting journalists had not been given anything to eat. Talk about PR!

Mandela is on many levels old-fashioned. Part of that is a result of having spent 27 years behind bars – when he was released from jail and journalists shoved a huge boom mike covered in a woolly wind sock towards him, Mandela looked alarmed and shouted, 'What is this?' And he asked the same question about a jelly bean – it was simply not in his realm of experience. But part of it is a tribute to his age. He was born in an era when men were far more polite and well mannered and, yes, a lot more sexist. But at the same time, Mandela manages to be extremely up-to-date and quite modern. He will tell you that men should help women around the house and proudly boasts that he can cook and clean with the best of them. He has also managed to advance the fight against AIDS, a commitment which very few men and women of his generation would be able to make.

Part of this mixture is an instinctive lack of guile. In many ways Mandela, the greatest statesman, is too good a man to be a great politician. He lacks that deceptive element in his personality. Much of what you see is what you get. And yet at the same time he is extremely disciplined and committed to his cause.

PROMISES AND LIES

Coupled with the royal and the Victorian is an absolute abhor-
rence of dishonesty. Quite simply Mandela is an extremely moral
man. He cannot abide lies and is truly a man of deep integrity, a
man of his word. At one time his relationship with IFP leader
Mangosuthu Buthelezi suffered a serious breakdown, partly
because the man had not kept his word. In the same vein, his
relationship with FW de Klerk was strained to the point that it
suffered an irretrievable breakdown because he was convinced
that the former apartheid leader had lied to him about his knowledge of the existence of government-sponsored 'Third Force' violence. He felt betrayed by De Klerk; and although at one point
the world fêted both leaders to the point of awarding a joint
Nobel Peace Prize, the pair never really managed to develop the
kind of chemistry Mandela had astonishingly achieved with De
Klerk's predecessor, PW Botha. De Klerk may have released
Mandela from jail, but as far as Mandela is concerned, it was
Botha who set the ball in motion. And in many ways the two
men have far more in common, including their age, than
Mandela and De Klerk. But the lesson in this is that once
Mandela feels betrayed by someone, he is quite capable of cutting
that person off for good.

Mandela is capable of forgiving many things. Often to his
peril he will overlook debilitating faults in people and give them
a second chance. But lie to him or betray him, and he will probably write you off for good. *He will more than likely catch you out
in a lie and if he does you are finished. You can get away with a lot of
things, but not with even the smallest of lies. Whenever things have
gone wrong with his relationships with other people, it is usually
because that person has broken his/her word or lied to him.*

A case in point is his relationship with former rugby supremo
Louis Luyt which was irreparably damaged after he subpoenaed
the President to appear in court. Mandela had ordered a judicial
inquiry into the affairs of rugby and Luyt as SARFU president,
was challenging the validity of that inquiry and the way in
which the President had set it up. Apart from the fact that it was

a sickening sight to see a man of Mandela's stature dragged into court for such a petty reason, it was what was said during the proceedings that changed things between them forever. Without going into too much detail, Luyt literally accused the President of lying. And that Mandela could simply not tolerate. The corners of his mouth went down and he fixed Luyt with that famous impassive look of stone. Since then things have never been the same between them. Mandela has stated publicly, both prior to and since that infamous court case, that he has great respect for Louis Luyt. This is based on Luyt's willingness to travel to Lusaka to talk to the ANC in the 1980s about the normalisation of sport. This incurred the wrath of the then government, the rugby fraternity and the Afrikaner nation. It was a very courageous step, one that Madiba admired, yet the court case probably changed their relationship. *This is personally a great sadness to me because I admire both men. I wish it could be different. Regardless of the souring relationship, Madiba never failed to show his good side. During the court case and afterwards he always went out of his way to greet Dr Luyt.*

There were also a few secretaries, personal assistants and various other staff who became casualties during Madiba's presidency for no other reason than that they failed to tell the truth. *Fortunately, my father held the same views about lying as Madiba and I was taught from the beginning never to lie to him. My sons are in the process of learning exactly the same and there are few things more valuable for a son to learn from his father.*

"...

A true story as told by
Nelson Mandela

When I visited Zimbabwe recently, I met a young lady of around
10 or 11. One day she came to me and said that all her friends in
her class were telling her that in my younger days I used to be a
very handsome man. I told her this was good to know. But then
she said, 'no, *now* I am talking about *now*. Now you are a very
ugly old man.'

... "

As mentioned in the preface, in this chapter Rory and Debora's paths started crossing more frequently. In addition to Rory's own observations Debora has added her own. It was at this period that Debora was strengthening her own relationship with the presidential couple and hence this chapter becomes more personal as Debora shares her own reflections alongside those of Rory's.

7

Mandela in Love

I must say I was very happy. I was very happy.
At my age I don't do things that I don't feel good
about. I'm no longer at the age where
I do things because I'm told to.
(Graça Machel on her marriage to Nelson Mandela.)

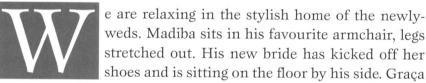

We are relaxing in the stylish home of the newly-weds. Madiba sits in his favourite armchair, legs stretched out. His new bride has kicked off her shoes and is sitting on the floor by his side. Graça Machel and Nelson Mandela have only been married for two weeks, but already their relationship is characterised by the kind of intimacy shared by couples who've known each other for a long time. It is not the setting one would associate with a head of state and his First Lady. Instead it is the relaxed environment of a couple enjoying a private moment far away from the glare of the public eye. Debora has just asked the President whether marriage will change his life in any way. Sipping his tea and pausing thoughtfully for a moment, he leans over with a wicked gleam in his eye and confides laughingly, 'Debora, I have only two priorities in my life right now. Number one, Graça, and number two – eating prawns in Mozambique.'

The President may be joking but his words contain a measure of truth. For a man whose life has been defined by politics, whose every decision has been based on a concern for the greater good, and where the personal has always been sacrificed for the political, it is only now in his eighties that he is seizing what's left of his life and making it his own. A colleague remarked recently that on reaching the grand old age of 80, Nelson Mandela teaches us all the cheery lesson that if you wait long enough, eventually true love and fame do come your way.

When Mandela first came out of prison he wouldn't touch prawns or crayfish, or any kind of seafood for that matter. It wasn't just that this type of food isn't in his framework of experience, it was also that he simply did not have time for life's little luxuries. Now, if given the chance, he will go into a lengthy description of just how good Graça is at getting the freshest and best prawns and crab from Maputo's fish markets and how much he enjoys eating them with a Portuguese peri-peri sauce. In fact, so much so, that he's instructed Graça's children to make sure that there's seafood available whenever he visits Mozambique, which is quite regularly these days. Also, any member of the Machel or Mandela families travelling from Maputo to Johannesburg will always be accompanied by a cooler-box full of prawns.

This absolute delight in the joys of Mozambican cuisine is really a metaphor for the change that's come about in the President. When he was first released from prison it was almost impossible to get Madiba to talk about anything personal. He was the ANC. When Mandela spoke about any matter, it was the ANC speaking. The ANC defined Mandela's character and provided his terms of reference. A loyal and disciplined member, there was hardly anything he ever said that wasn't a political statement or a reflection of organisational policy. He never dwells on the fact that he spent 27 years in jail, deprived of the chance to see his children grow up and to develop a proper relationship with his then wife, Winnie Madikizela-Mandela. If he ever felt pain and anger over what happened to him, it was never expressed. The only thing that mattered was the struggle, the fight for freedom and the liberation of South Africa and if that meant 27 years in jail, then so be it. In fact up until his marriage to Graça Machel, the only time he had ever publicly expressed any emotion about his time behind bars was when he returned to Robben Island for the first time after his release. It was in 1994, prior to South Africa's first all-race elections. And it was here that Mandela, soon to become president, spoke publicly about the last time he saw his mother alive. There were tears in his eyes as he recalled how he watched her leave the prison and walk down the path towards the ferry that would take her across Table Bay back to Cape Town. As the figure got smaller and smaller, he somehow sensed that this would be the last time he would see her alive. She died not long afterwards and he was never granted permission to attend her funeral. But even that was all part of the sacrifice that had to be made for the struggle. All that was personal was sacrificed for the sake of a greater political good.

THE LONELIEST MAN IN THE WORLD

But since Mandela's release from jail, there has been a healthy development towards recognising that it's okay to have something special just for himself that does not necessarily fit the struggle ideal. It became clear that Madiba was hankering after something more following his divorce from Winnie Madikizela-Mandela. The divorce finally took place in 1996 after much ducking and diving by Madikizela-Mandela. It was a particularly uncomfortable time for Steyn and the other bodyguards, who had no real wish to be privy to something as painful and private as this obviously was. *It was such a personal matter and the children, Zinzi and Zenani, had actually become quite good friends by that stage. I could only imagine how painful the divorce had become for them, having waited so long to be finally reunited with their father. I saw this whole matter as a personal concern of the President and purposefully did not become involved any further than my official duties required.*

Winnie had deliberately failed to arrive in court when the judge was supposed to hear her case for alimony. And so, as was his judicial right, the judge ruled in her absence. This meant that there was no need to hear arguments in favour of her case.

After the divorce the President rarely saw his former wife. He was always extremely cordial to her in public and there were many within the ANC who still hoped that there would be a reconciliation.

A SECRET SPRING IN HIS STEP AND A SPARKLE IN HIS EYE

His choice of Graça Machel was not, by ANC standards, the perfect one. Although Graça has the right struggle credentials, she is not South African. A fact that led to a certain amount of xenophobia amongst some ANC members, especially from the Women's League, who felt that Mandela should marry one of his own. But after years of doing the right thing for the struggle and South Africa, Madiba refused to take these concerns seriously and followed his heart instead. And the result is a romance that was billed as one of the last great love affairs of the twentieth century.

Initially their relationship was conducted with great secrecy and often with several guardians around in case anybody got the wrong idea. It was such a closely guarded secret that only a select few were let in on the delicious story.

It began when Mandela was still only legally separated from Madikizela-Mandela, and with the divorce pending he did not want Graça Machel's name dragged through the mud. But the very nature of the job demanded that some of Mandela's protectors had to be bought in on the secret and were specially instructed by Mandela to tell no one, even though they knew of this budding romance from as early as 1995.

One of their earliest secret meetings took place in easily one of the most romantic settings in the world – Paris. Mandela was attending Bastille Day celebrations in the French capital in its summer of 1996, and on several evenings Graça visited him at the presidential guesthouse and had meals with him as well as accompanying him (separately of course) to one or two of the more intimate official functions. On the occasions that they went to official functions together, the guards were instructed to make sure she left the place unnoticed. 'But,' says his personal assistant Zelda la Grange, 'we didn't realise that romance was in the air at this stage. We just thought that Mrs Machel was a friend of the President.' But there were those on the presidential staff who definitely thought otherwise, especially when the media reported that the couple were spotted strolling through the streets of Paris holding hands! Says Zelda, 'This was not true. They never held hands in public in Paris.'

Those on the President's staff who had not been brought in on the secret by then could easily guess that something was up. The couple would organise romantic trysts whenever Graça was in Johannesburg. They would meet either at her house in Woodmead (she was staying with a friend there) or otherwise Mandela would fetch her and they would spend time at his Houghton residence. It was not long before Graça Machel won the approval of everybody on the President's team. Bodyguard Quintin Henwick says, 'There was no doubt that it was love. You just had to look in the President's eyes to see the sparkle there.'

The time the new couple spent together was extremely limited. Not only did they have to keep their relationship a secret but they both had extremely busy schedules. He was after all the world's most favoured leader, sought after by presidents and pop stars. And she was a senior member of the United Nations Children's Fund (UNICEF), which meant that she travelled the globe as an ambassador for this cause. In addition, Graça ran an educational centre for children back in her home base of Maputo, which took up much of her time.

Despite the distance and the constraints of having to conduct a relationship in secret, the romance blossomed. The couple began a practice of never ending a day without talking to each other. The President would not go to bed if he had not phoned Graça, no matter where they were in the world.

The presidential courtship continued in an almost teenage fashion. *I recall us having to go to Sandton City to buy chocolates for Graça at the end of 1996. Such a simple act, a simple exercise turned into pandemonium.* Mandela, you see, insisted on personally choosing and buying the chocolates himself. Anyone on his huge staff would have been more than willing to perform this most basic of acts, but he would have none of that. He was the suitor and would not have thought to leave so important a task to anyone else. So the bodyguards had to sweep through the plush shopping centre with sniffer dogs (if there was sufficient notice), clear the area of any potential danger and then keep the crowds, who mobbed Mandela as soon as they realised who was doing the shopping, at bay. Such pandemonium! But it was nice to see this common, romantic touch. And it wasn't just a one-off thing. Mandela got into the habit of visiting the shopping centre to purchase chocolates, flowers and other romantic gifts for Graça. Never once did he delegate this task to any of his staff. He was determined to do it himself even if it meant turning everything upside down. *He did all the romantic things a man in love does – shopping for jewellery, flowers, selecting gifts. But it was not easy to go shopping for Graça. He really is a true romantic. He reminded me of a teenager with his first girlfriend.*

In addition to securing the shopping centre, the bodyguards also had to pay advance visits to the jewellers, florists and chocolatiers. So important was Mandela's name that most stores would not let him pay for his purchases. However, the President did not like this and would always insist on paying. His retort was always that, 'I cannot come back and buy something else unless you let me pay for this.' Hence the bodyguards conducted advance visits of a different kind. They would inform the store manager ahead of time that the President would be coming, swearing him or her to secrecy and explaining that he was not to be given anything free.

THE SECRET IS OUT

But these secret romantic meetings could not continue forever. The media was speculating furiously on the possibility of a relationship and already at this stage talk of marriage was in the air. Eventually in September 1996, the couple felt that it was time to go public. A story was deliberately leaked to the media, which Mandela's office then confirmed officially a day later. Certain journalists and photographers from major national newspapers were informed and the couple was photographed strolling hand in hand through Houghton's greenery. It was true: Nelson Mandela was in love with Graça Machel. She was to be given the title of 'Official Companion' and would accompany him on state visits and other functions where her schedule permitted it. To their delight, news of this love affair was met with widespread support from all but the most sour of South Africans.

But despite intense media speculation there was still no talk of marriage. And not because Mandela didn't want this. He pestered Graça for months to give in but she was firm; she simply did not want to marry, chiefly out of concern for her children and preserving the name of her late husband. So instead, in a thoroughly modern relationship, Graça became his official companion on his various trips around the world. It's hard to think of another presidential couple getting away with such an arrangement. Imagine the scandal it would cause elsewhere in the world. However most people were delighted that he'd found happiness.

Once the relationship between the couple had become public, there was no stopping the President's ardour. Mandela would insist on going personally to Johannesburg International Airport to fetch Graça or drop her off. *It bordered on the ridiculous because Madiba would insist on going right to the plane, even going inside the cabin to meet her. Can you imagine the chaos this caused? People couldn't believe their eyes, not knowing whether to drop their luggage and rush to shake his hand or simply keep a discreet distance. And how do you keep a discreet distance inside a jumbo jet's fuselage?* Eventually practical considerations took over and Steyn managed to persuade Mandela to wait in a private airport lounge (dubbed the Maputo room by airport staff) while the protocol officers fetched Graça from the plane and escorted her to the VIP room. *This turned out to be a much better arrangement and they could also have their privacy while the luggage was fetched.* Then whenever they had to say goodbye to each other it was like a physical wrench. On the extremely rare occasions when Graça managed to persuade Mandela not to travel with her to the airport, he would come out of the house with her and they would kiss like teenagers, unashamedly, in front of the entire waiting security contingent. 'She would get into her car and he would continue to wave and blow kisses until the vehicle was out of sight,' says Henwick.

Seeing the presidential couple greet each other on board public aircraft wasn't the only sight South Africans were treated to. The pair was regularly seen strolling through the leafy suburb of Houghton, hand in hand, greeting neighbours. And in Maputo they became a permanent fixture on many a weekend. Both Mozambique and South Africa thrilled in this unusual but charming romance.

There were, however, still one or two awkward moments with the President's former wife. On one of their first public appearances as a couple, Winnie Madikizela-Mandela showed up uninvited. The occasion was a ceremony at a Soweto school. Mandela and Graça were sitting on a stage, the ceremony well under way, when Winnie swept in late. She was not supposed to be there and no arrangements had been made for her, as officials hurriedly tried to find her a chair. Mandela stared stonily ahead the whole time. But sensitive as ever to Graça's feelings, he made a point of holding her hand throughout the entire occasion.

There was still one thorn in their flesh: friend and activist Anglican Archbishop Desmond Tutu took it upon himself to regularly berate Mandela for setting a bad example to the youth by living together instead of marrying.

After a while the pressure on the couple became so intense that instead of greeting Mandela, Tutu would simply say, 'Until when?' at every opportunity. As has been noted, it wasn't Mandela who didn't want to tie the knot. The reluctance was on Graça's side because she is an independent woman who was still committed to keeping alive the name of her late husband, Samora Machel, who had died in a sinister plane crash just inside the border of South Africa.

RECONCILING THE PAST

The Truth and Reconciliation Commission (TRC) was probing the death of Graça's former husband, the then Mozambican President, Samora Machel in the plane crash that had occurred in 1986. The theory they were investigating was that the plane had been diverted off course by a decoy beacon, forcing it to crash just along the South African/Mozambican border. Graça had done her own extensive work into the causes of the 'accident' and her testimony was crucial to the success of the TRC's work. She was convinced that the crash was no accident. Mandela had requested permission to sit with Graça during the testimony. But not even the President could be afforded special privileges. Ever a stickler for principle, TRC Chairperson Archbishop Desmond Tutu had to turn this down. The hearing was closed to the public. This was not because they had anything to hide but rather because this was only an initial investigation and statements not based on fact could become prejudicial. Tutu told Mandela he could wait in a room next door 'to comfort his girlfriend'. After discussing it with Graça, it was agreed that Mandela wouldn't sit next door and they would meet up later. But like all other victims of apartheid atrocities, when the time finally came it was extremely difficult and emotionally painful for Graça to relive those memories. She broke down in tears during her testimony. Her bodyguards managed to get word of this through to the President via Steyn and Mandela's secretary, Zelda la Grange. Mandela had been on a brief trip outside Johannesburg and all formalities at the Air Force base were immediately cut short so that he could land and return home at once to be with her – but not before stopping off to buy a beautiful bunch of flowers in Woodmead.

Intense media speculation continued to surround this world-famous romance. Mandela was constantly badgered by the media. Ever the gentleman, he fobbed off these questions with a series of standard replies, including the fact that in his culture it was not appropriate for a person younger than him to ask questions of such a personal nature. And finally he would simply quip, 'Ask Graça!' A hint of *who* was really holding things up.

A WEDDING IN THE AIR

But the rumours continued and there were persistent reports that a wedding was going to happen 'any day now'.

The South African public wanted nothing more than a wedding, which they were convinced would be the equivalent of a royal marriage, so impressive was Mandela's status around the globe. What they didn't know was that by 1998 Mandela had finally convinced Graça to marry him. And just as their pre-marital relationship was characterised by unconventional living arrangements, so too was their marriage. The old Mandela would have thought long and hard about the political implications of a marriage and would probably have decided to hold a very public ceremony that would have served as a unifying force for the South African nation. But with a new, more personal approach to life, Madiba and Graça decided that their relationship was an intensely private affair and that they would celebrate it by having a wedding that was theirs and theirs alone. Some of Mandela's happiest moments were in the planning of that special day. He seemed to be having the time of his life as he went about fooling his own staff and the rest of the world. Everything had to be organised with the utmost secrecy. A special jeweller was selected and sworn to secrecy. Mandela conducted his first meeting with him in Pretoria. Zelda remembers thinking at the time that Mandela seemed to have a very conspiratorial look about him that day. 'I was a little surprised that he didn't explain why the jeweller was there as he always gave background information on most appointments and the relevance of meetings. And I was even more surprised when they met in the garden as if they deliberately did not want any over-eager ears listening in. A thought crossed my mind that maybe 'Khulu' was organising a wedding, but then I dismissed this because I was sure I would have managed to detect other signs of such a ceremony.'

In order to keep the public off the scent of the trail, the jeweller later met the couple in a private suite at the Mount Nelson Hotel in Cape Town instead of at his shop. Here the wedding rings were carefully selected. The printing of the simple red and white order of service was kept to the last minute and published without a date so that nobody would guess the truth.

Then there was the matter of the wedding dress: a slightly more difficult thing to keep secret. Bodyguards Quintin Henwick and Popi Lukhele were the ones given the task of accompanying Graça to her fittings. For about six weeks, the pair went with her on a weekly basis to a dressmaker in the centre of Johannesburg. The gown was an exquisite white and gold number that looked every inch bridal. Graça realised on the second visit that the bodyguards may have guessed the truth, so she told them that the dress was for her godchild's wedding. They didn't believe her for a moment, but ever discreet, as their profession demands, they played along, telling nobody of their suspicions. By this time Steyn and Zelda were also growing increasingly suspicious. *There were numerous visits to Xilembene (Graça's ancestral home) and the Transkei. We thought that these constant trips may have been to gain approval from both families, but again it was just not the done thing to say anything.*

Things were going extremely well. Then two days before the big day, Johannesburg's weekly newspaper, *The Star,* ran a story under a banner headline that Graça Machel and Mandela would marry in secret on his birthday. The denials flew thick and fast. Mandela's office had not been informed and so the presidential spokesmen put their necks on the line by stating over and over again that there was no wedding. Later they were accused of lying, but in fact they didn't know until literally hours before the ceremony took place. Steyn's opinion is that they should simply have stayed out of it. *'The Office has no comment as this is a private and personal matter,'* should have been the response.

Zelda says, 'We as staff members were upset with the news-papers. Even if these papers confirmed our suspicions, we would have preferred it to be a secret even to ourselves, until the 18th.'

Graça says that the secrecy was absolutely necessary. She explains that if they had had a public wedding they would have had to invite thousands of people and that would not have been possible. 'We could not invite all the friends and because of that we would have hurt some people. We decided to treat everybody equally and not tell anyone until after the wedding took place.' On the subject of marriage itself, Graça is a little less circumspect, almost poetic. 'You know that marriage is the only thing in life where you really make a choice, did you know that? You choose everything. You choose the person you want to get married to, you choose the day, you choose the hour, you choose how you want to be dressed, you choose who you want to perform the ceremony, you even choose how many people you want to be around. You can choose everything, it has to be that special moment. You don't choose when you want to be born, or when you are going to die, but marriage is the only thing you can choose every single detail of what you want, that's why it's so special for everybody.'

And certainly Graça's personal choices were evident in every aspect of the momentous occasion. Two days before the big day, staff had still not been brought in on the secret. Mandela's spokesman, Parks Mankahlana, was vigorously denying in the media that a marriage was going to take place. Zelda remembers phoning Graça's daughter Josina (who had become a great friend) to find out if anything was up. 'I'll be furious if there's a wedding,' she teased and making a big joke of their conversation, Josina denied everything. But even Josina knew nothing, as the children had also been left out of the secret. Zelda is the curious type and the suspicion was killing her. For this reason she had to exhaust all resources to get to the bottom of it – but to no avail. "Josina told me later that her mother only told her days before the ceremony, but made her promise not to tell anyone, and I was anyone." The strange requests continued. Mandela asked to meet leaders from all the different faiths and the jewellery man paid a final visit.

THE BIG DAY

The night before the big day, Mandela called Steyn to one side saying, 'Rory, there is going to be a private ceremony here this afternoon. Rabbi Harris will be coming.' Still no word of a wedding was mentioned. The appointed time arrived. There were only six people there to witness the occasion: Steyn, presidential spokesman Parks Mankahlana, Mrs Harris, a photographer, a cameraman and journalist Jon Qwelane (invited to record the occasion for posterity). The Rabbi blessed the couple and then there was tea and cake. But still nobody officially mentioned the word wedding.

Saturday 18 July dawned. It was the President's birthday. His 80th birthday. Zelda received a traditional early morning call from her boss to get someone on the line for him. 'It's your birthday,' she chided gently. 'You're not supposed to be phoning anyone, people must phone you.' And then not realising the deeper significance of her next words, 'I hope it's the most beautiful day of your life.' In a rare moment of personal intimacy, the President hesitated for a moment and then said, 'You don't know how much those words mean to me. I can assure you it really will be the best day of my life.' Zelda recalls that this was totally unlike the President. 'It really was one of only two occasions that he said something so personal.' He was going to celebrate his birthday surrounded by his children and grandchildren at the gracious presidential residence in Pretoria. There was tea and cake and generally a lot of merriment and this went on well after lunchtime. Outside the residence journalists crammed against the gate anxiously trying to gauge if this was indeed a wedding. Then a few minutes before the couple was due to return to Houghton, the President called his family into the lounge and told them he would be getting married to Graça Machel in just a few hours' time. They had not been told before because the pair wanted it to be a secret. So private was the wedding that not even their own children attended it. It was a shrewd move not to inform them, because members of the Mandela clan were inundated with queries about a possible wedding and they were able to truthfully say that no such thing was planned. After the announcement, there were shrieks of joy and the group broke out into a traditional African wedding song, meaning 'It is agreed', as they followed the pair to their car.

Standing outside the gates, the media heard this song with great suspicion. There was huge confusion as various different rumours circulated. The President and Graça had already married. 'No', said someone else, 'it happened last night and they only informed the children today.' Then somebody shouted that it was still going to happen at Houghton and everyone should rush over there. This coincided with a media alert on alpha-page stating that Deputy President Thabo Mbeki would be making an important announcement in Pretoria in about an hour's time. The media then rushed over to Mbeki's residence. But it turned out that this was a decoy, a specially devised plan to get the journalists off the trail and away from Houghton.

Literally half an hour before the ceremony took place, a new rumour started circulating that something was indeed up in Houghton, as Mbeki had just arrived there rather than at his official residence. Everyone jumped into their cars and raced off, breaking every traffic law and travelling at terribly high speeds.

Back in Houghton things were a lot calmer. The specially invited guests, no more than sixteen, started arriving. Very few of them had been let in on the secret – they'd simply been invited to a special ceremony at Mandela's home on his 80th birthday. But the minute they got there, everybody knew that this was no ordinary birthday party. Chairs had been arranged in a semicircle around a special table in the lounge. And Johannesburg's Chief Magistrate Charlton Bashe, who would perform all the legalities, was present.

'Mandela, a man whose playground is the entire world, could easily have married his Graça in a blaze of publicity, with the world's media networks in attendance and the globe's high and mighty worshipping at the couple's feet,' says Jon Qwelane. But instead a few close friends, Steyn, Chris Ngcobo and Zelda and the household staff who were there to help with the arrangements, the invited guests and five clerics (obviously including Archbishop Desmond Tutu and his wife) from the major religious dominations of South Africa, were the only witnesses.

There was Walter Sisulu, one of the great figures of the liberation struggle and Madiba's fellow Rivonia-trialist and Robben Island inmate, together with his wife, Albertina. Sisulu and Mandela have been friends for more than half a century. A bond that was obviously cemented by the long years behind bars together before their release, just a few months apart. His presence at this important moment in the President's personal life was a given.

Next to arrive was Thabo Mbeki, then ANC president and heir apparent to the Mandela throne. Beaming from ear to ear and sporting his usual distinguished attire, he arrived hand in hand with his wife, Zanele, clad in emerald-green. Another struggle stalwart to arrive was Mandela's personal advisor and prison cellmate Ahmed 'Kathy' Kathrada. His attire reflected the President's own love of the informal as he arrived wearing an open-necked shirt and tweeds. Graça's two brothers had been flown in from Mozambique, accompanied by a government official from a neighbouring state. And Mandela's sister had left her home in Qunu specially for the occasion. They were the only family members given the green light to attend. Other ANC members in attendance included Justice Minister Dullah Omar, who bore the distinction of being one of the first civilians allowed to visit Mandela in his last years at Victor Verster Prison. He was accompanied by his wife. And then there was Jacob Zuma, deputy president of the ANC and now of South Africa. The only black cloud was the unpleasant tidings he brought with him. He would have to leave the happy occasion early , as there had been a dramatic upsurge of political violence in the battered town of Richmond. Apart from these people, the only 'outsiders' were HRH Prince Bandar El Saoud of Saudi Arabia and Yusuf Surtee, friend and draper to the President. The joyful Archbishop made sure that Prince Bandar was welcomed into the small community and cheekily informed everyone that they had better treat the royal visitor kindly, because 'he should give us oil'.

With the guests all seated, the ceremony could now take place. Qwelane sums it up by saying it was, 'the simplicity of the wedding, especially for a ceremony spread over two days, that was perhaps its most poignant force.' For a man revered universally as one of the century's truly great leaders and statesmen, there was no lavish feast or wasteful expenditure. 'No slaughtered beasts,' adds Qwelane. 'No feasting, no praise singers. Just what the President and his bride desired, and just what they got.' And for Mandela it was a double celebration, a wedding and a birthday. And the best present he could have ever wished for was of course the hand of his beloved Graça.

The groom was the first to arrive downstairs, resplendent in a black and gold 'Madiba shirt'. 'Nelson Mandela is the very essence of charisma, changing the atmosphere and scenario in a room by his mere presence. His grey hairs, a result of age and years of pain and suffering, lend an authoritative air of sagacity to the man,' writes Qwelane.

And as he stepped into the lounge, the warmth of his brilliant smile literally, to borrow a cliché, lit up the entire room. Then looking every inch the beautiful bride, Graça Machel came slowly down the staircase of the house. Mandela gazed up at her adoringly; she smiled contentedly. This was indeed a truly happy couple. Qwelane is even more generous with his praise when it comes to Graça. 'Let there be no doubt that Graça is a very beautiful woman. Tall, regal, slim and statuesque. A sculptor's dream model, if ever there was one. Her beautiful smile reveals a gleaming set of white teeth and lights up a room.'

Wearing the hip-hugging gold and cream dress that had been the subject of all those secret journeys to the dressmaker, she walked slowly over to Mandela and clasped his arm. First there was the legal ceremony. The couple signed the wedding register on a specially set up ornamental table. The marriage was recorded on a simple white form: a standard government marriage licence, no different from any other. Only this certificate bears the famous Mandela signature and cemented the most talked-about wedding in South Africa's history. Then it was time for the more traditional exchange of vows conducted by Methodist Bishop Mvume Dandala (Madiba is a Methodist) and Archbishop Desmond Tutu. Like many grooms before him, Mandela fumbled momentarily in his pocket searching for the rings. And like many other grooms, he needed a little prodding from his bride to produce the goods. They were finally located and moments later South Africa had a First Lady. 'When the couple exchanged their vows, they did so with no hesitation and no tears,' remembers Zelda, 'but it was the rest of us that got all emotional. Most of us had tears in our eyes as they said "I Do", it was hard to believe that this was at long last happening. And even harder to believe that we were all witnessing this moment. The sight of Madiba getting married is not the stuff of everyday normality. But we were there to witness it and we appreciated this opportunity more than anything in the world.'

For Steyn, who had been one step behind Mandela for close on five years now, it was a day he would never forget. *While I was standing there, I continually had this sense of profound privilege to be witnessing it because there were so few of us and also because of the suddenness of the whole occasion. The previous night, the President hadn't explained it to me and it was only while the Jewish blessing was happening that I realised that this was his wedding. So while it was happening, I kept thinking, 'wow, am I really here?' I felt deeply honoured. I felt such immense joy, because I had seen over the years just how much happiness Graça brought him. I can honestly say I felt incredibly happy and the last thing I did before I left that night, was congratulate Mam Graça and thank her for the happiness she'd brought to our President.*

For the rest of those privileged enough to attend this momentous occasion, it was a memory to be treasured forever. Everyone was overjoyed that Mandela had at last found happiness. Zelda la Grange says that before Mandela met Graça, 'It would break her heart to see him sitting alone at night. There he would be, in his favourite armchair in Qunu, with a blanket over his legs, all alone. It was upsetting to see him sitting all by himself on overseas visits or in Qunu, at his huge dining room table eating breakfast, lunch and dinner.' This famous man, courted and celebrated around the globe, was all on his own in his more intimate moments. But afterwards, agrees Zelda, he was like a different man. There was more balance to his life in dealing with personal things with Graça around. And having a wife made a huge difference in his ability to deal with the sophisticated world of the nineties. For although Mandela was a world-famous man, 27 years behind bars meant he had missed out on acquiring many of the social niceties demanded of people these days. He was used to doing things on his own. 'But now,' adds Zelda, 'he had a wife which meant that he was able to deal with certain social occasions a lot better because of her. She is the ultimate hostess and will attend to details that Madiba (and most men) will not think of. He asks her for advice on things all the time, especially when it comes to dealing with the children. They communicate about everything.'

I am very grateful for Tutu's interference: it was right for them to get married. And the irrepressible Archbishop made no attempt to hide his enthusiasm that Mandela 'had at last made an honest woman of Graça!' He really was the life and soul of that party, cracking jokes at every available opportunity. A few minutes after the ceremony had been completed, Tutu slipped his copy of the order of service over to the couple and asked for an autograph. He looked up at the bride as she signed it Graça Machel and said, 'Hey, have you already forgotten your new surname?' And then when the President had appended his signature he also had something to say. Winking mischievously, he said *'Ndiya kuyithengisa!'*, which jokingly meant that he was going to auction the programme now that he had their signatures on it.

For someone who had resisted marriage and the Archbishop's advice for so long, Graça Machel really was the epitome of the radiant bride. She said afterwards, 'I must tell you, I was very happy. I was very happy. At my age I don't do things that I don't feel good about. I'm no longer at the age where I do things because I'm told to.'

The woman who has put the sparkle back into the Madiba's eyes and a spring in his step is fiercely independent and will continue to uphold this independence. You will not always see Graça at Mandela's side at official functions, for South Africa's new First Lady is determined to continue her work in Maputo. Graça will also continue to travel around the world in her role as an ambassador for UNICEF; and the couple will still maintain residences in both South Africa and Mozambique. Prior to the marriage, Graça would visit Madiba on average about two weeks out of every month, while the President would often sneak up to Maputo for a weekend of prawns and sun. These arrangements continued as if nothing had changed.

But perhaps the most remarkable thing of all is just how comfortable Mandela is with these arrangements. Particularly given the fact that he comes from a generation where men were quite firmly the head of the household. Graça could have chosen to give up her job and live the life of easy luxury she would have enjoyed as South Africa's First Lady. But instead she remains a working woman, a mother and very much her own person, despite being part of a couple. *To see her in her home in Maputo is to witness a woman totally at ease with herself. This is a modern woman, a former cabinet minister for 13 years, down to earth, a real mother and also a homemaker.*

Graça Machel's modern approach to life, love and career began long before she met Nelson Mandela. Born Graça Simbine, she is a university graduate who's conversant in four languages and who joined Frelimo's armed struggle for independence and was a freedom fighter.

She married Samora Machel a few months after Mozambican independence in 1975 and was the liberated country's first Education Minister, a post that she still held at the time of her husband's death in 1986. Together this talented and charismatic couple believed that they could bring peace to Mozambique throughout the years of destabilisation and then help the country to grow economically.

Then came the Mbuzini plane crash. It was an event that shattered the Machel household and changed Graça Machel forever. For well over a decade now it has defined who she is and what she wants out of life. So devastated was the widow that she wore only black for five years. Graça now says that were it not for a comment passed by her youngest son, Malinga, she might never have taken off her mourning clothes. She describes how it happened. 'One day I was tidying up my bedroom and Malinga came in. He was sitting on my bed and I opened my wardrobe. At that time everything was black. So he looked at this and said, "You know Mama?"

'I said, "yes?" He said, "the other day I tried to remember what you looked like before you were wearing black and I couldn't remember you. All the images of you that I have are in black."

'I said, "no, what do you mean?"

'He said, "It's true. I even closed my eyes and I tried to think how my mama looked before she was in black and I just couldn't remember."

'So I understood what the message was.' Graça hugged her youngest son and told him it was okay and that she would change.

'He then said, "No, I didn't mean anything, because I know you have your problems." But I understood the message. I told him that I promised to change; he should just give me some time. He was saying that the only mother he knew was a mourning mother, not the one who could smile, who could be everything, all these things. So I realised that without meaning to, I was doing harm to my own children.'

Graça may have changed her mourning attire but the pain inside her still is deep.

She is convinced that the crash was no accident and has dedicated her life to tracking down her husband's killers. Even if justice is not seen in her lifetime, she says, her children have vowed to carry on the hunt. For the first year after the plane crash, Graça was too traumatised to fly anywhere. The Tupolev 134 crashed shortly after the pilot instructed his passengers to fasten their seatbelts. And even today, every time the 'fasten seatbelt' sign lights up and a plane begins the descent for landing, Graça is haunted by visions of what her late husband's last moments alive must have been like. The crash is not a subject Graça will talk about easily and she has often said that she made the decision a long time ago that life must go on.

AMAZING GRAÇA

Debora first met Graça Machel at Mandela's Houghton residence. The meeting was friendly but a little stiff; the presidential residence does not lend itself to informality. And the fact that we were discussing the circumstances around the death of her former husband did not help the situation much either. It is still a traumatic subject for Graça and at one point she was reduced to tears, tears that were gently wiped away by Madiba. Ever the dignified statesman, he responded to the situation with deep sensitivity and generously used the occasion to pay tribute to Samora Machel's leadership and vision as a true son of Africa.

The next meeting was at her Maputo residence. She was barefoot and wearing a simple white T-shirt teamed with a red and black wrap-around skirt: this is the environment she clearly feels most comfortable in. Although Samora Machel never lived in this house, his powerful presence is evident in the giant black and white photograph of him that dominates the lounge. But it is still very much Graça's home, from the exquisite marbled floors to the simple African artwork, her stylish taste is evident everywhere. 'I love natural light,' she kept stressing and complained that Madiba's Houghton home was too dark. That has since changed as the couple bought a new house in Houghton and this time it is full of natural light, elegant tiled floors and an uncluttered, minimalist décor.

In her Maputo home the drink is chilled Portuguese white wine, dinner is delicious Mozambican cuisine and the talk is of Mozambican politics, investigations into the Machel crash and her children. A charming mixture of Latin and African, Graça is a delightful lunch companion and a lot easier to talk to away from the public glare.

Graça is an intensely private person, seldom giving public interviews and carefully guarding her personal life. Even now that the pair have married, she sheds very little light on their relationship.

She will tell you that while she had no intention of ever remarrying, a point she has made over and over again in public, she adds that 'Only a very special person, as Madiba is, could make me get married again.'

Asked once in a *60 Minutes* interview whether it entered her head that Mandela was an eligible bachelor again following his divorce from Winnie Madikizela-Mandela, she became tightlipped once again. 'I had a kind of relationship with Madiba after his divorce, but even then I was not intending to marry him. But that's a second person I don't want to discuss, that's Winnie. All I can say is that I came into Madiba's life at a time when she was completely out of his life. There was of course a legal process to formalise, but I could only be involved with Madiba when he was already a free man and I mean that he was no longer involved with her. Although they still had paper as husband and wife, he had nothing to do with her. That's why I could get involved with him.'

I press Graça a little further as to exactly when and how they fell in love. All she'll say in her charming Portuguese accent is that, 'How did we meet in terms of eye to eye, that we have something clinging between the two of us, this is our secret.'

What Graça will tell you is that although she does not like comparisons between Samora Machel and Nelson Mandela, she does believe that she's been married to the two tallest trees in Africa. And she concedes that perhaps what drew them together was a certain loneliness within the hectic pace of their lives. 'Of course we talked and we realise that both of us had been lonely. It is true, but more important than being lonely, is that we had both suffered in life. And if you are lucky as we are, to get a very happy moment, you will enjoy it much, much better than before.

You had the experience of what it is to suffer, what's pain, that's why this relationship is really so, so sweet. It's really sweet, it's because both of us have known what is pain. We can appreciate much better what it means to be together and to have someone who really, really loves you. So it's different and it's much sweeter than probably, you know, when you are very young. When you are 20 years old, you have all these dreams, it's just dreams, but one thing is reality which you can touch.'

Another reality is the families that surround both of them. The Machel family is extremely close, and, as previously mentioned, was one of the reasons Graça was reluctant to marry Mandela sooner. Since the death of their father, the children (five from Samora's previous marriage and two of her own) have surrounded her in a kind of protective love. But unlike many of the offspring of great leaders, they have none of the usual airs and graces. They are down to earth and enjoy an easy but intellectually stimulating relationship with their mother. Josina, the youngest, who bears a remarkable physical likeness to her late father, jokes with her mother, spending the time making witty retorts about many of the world's leaders. Graça is a little disillusioned with politics, believing that the Mozambican parliament has not accorded her husband his proper place in history. But she confides that she does not like to pass on her frustrations to Madiba, who is an optimist who tends to look for the good in people.

When she does speak of Mandela it is always in the most glowing of terms. She refers to him as and calls him 'Madiba', his Xhosa title.

Their relationship in many ways is like that of any normal couple. They have to cope with the routine schedules of running a busy household. Mandela supports four of his grandchildren who actually live with him. (He has 26 grandchildren and four great-grandchildren.) One day when I popped in for a visit, I was greeted by two young children sliding down the banisters of the family home and collapsing at my feet in a fit of giggles. The next minute their grandfather appeared and shaking his head said to me, 'Debora, make sure you only have two children. They can be so noisy and so expensive too! It just never ends, one day I give them money for a bus trip to the Kruger Park and the next day the school sends a note to say they need more money to pay for another school outing somewhere else.'

They too have their lovers' tiffs. Once, while I was visiting the Houghton residence, Mandela got up to close a window that was letting in cold air. Graça said, 'Oh Madiba, relax and sit down, you should have let me do that.' Mandela tried to defend his position but, eventually in the face of such stubborness, gave up laughing. 'Don't fight me now,' he warned, 'otherwise Debora will write that I don't believe in the equality of the sexes.' But above all it is a relationship of deep love and respect. They adore each other, with Mandela calling her 'darling' and seizing every opportunity to express his affection physically. It is Graça who also helps keep Madiba young. Straight after their marriage the couple went on a state visit to Brazil. During the official welcome Brazilian women dressed only in G-strings performed the samba for the newly-weds, much to Madiba's intense embarrassment. He kept turning to Graça saying, 'Darling, do you see what they're wearing?'

Graça on the other hand was completely unperturbed and calmly informed Madiba that it was perfectly natural in Brazil. On another occasion Mandela was rushing off to meet Prince Charles and the Spice Girls back home in South Africa. He turned to me and said, 'Debora, by the way, who are these Spice Girls?' Graça just threw her head back and roared with laughter, 'Oh Madiba, you had better speak to your grandchildren about them.'

WHO'S THE BOSS?

It is obvious that Mandela enjoyes having a wife; someone who is a friend, but also someone to share in domestic duties. And becoming part of his life, Graça made sure that he dded not overstretch himself.

During his presidency, she would conspire with Zelda la Grange in ensuring that his schedule was not too heavy.

Mandela in Love ═══ 201

Mandela, however, soon got wise to this and would routinely give her the slip, sometimes using his bodyguards to do the 'dirty work'. For example, there would be times that he was supposed to be resting when he would sneak out of the house to attend to some or other business. 'Rory,' he would say to Steyn, 'if Mam' Graça calls, just tell her I'm around or sleeping.' Then off he would go. And if Mandela wanted to organise something without Graça catching on, he would start speaking to his guards in Afrikaans in front of her, a language she has no knowledge of at all. This happened on one occasion when Mandela wanted to surprise Graça by visting her in Xilembene, while he was enjoying his New Year holiday in Maputo. She had expressly forbidden him to go up there because there were too many mosquitoes. *'Rory, jy moet asseblief reël vir daardie groot ding wat kan vlieg sodat ek vir Mama kan verras!'* ('Rory you must please arrange for that big thing that flies (a helicopter) so that I can surprise Mama!')

But while Graça manages to get her way with many things, she had no influence when it came to the President's style of dressing. The official photograph of the couple was taken at their Houghton residence in October 1998. And there to witness it was of course protection team leader Rory Steyn. *I remember Mama asking Madiba whether he shouldn't wear a suit. 'No,' he replied, 'people know me like this.' He was of course wearing his trademark Madiba shirt and she was dressed in her favourite style of African-type dress with puffed-out sleeves and traditional motifs.*

LOVED BY ALL

It seems that Graça Machel manages to charm people wherever the couple goes. She quickly won the hearts of all the presidential staff, particularly the bodyguards who were assigned to her once she had become First Lady. Like her husband, she too made sure that she treated everyone with equanimity and respect. Just as the protectors grew accustomed to calling the President *'Tata'*, Graça was addressed simply as *'Mam' Graça'.*

With Graça in his life, presidential trips to Mozambique became more and more frequent. And just recently the

Mozambican government presented Mandela with some prime real estate, on a corner stand in Maputo. It is here that the couple are building another house that they will share during his Mozambican visits. Graça's house is built on several levels and the President's bad knee just doesn't allow him to move up and down all those stairs with ease.

One of the quaint aspects of going to Mozambique is fetching Mandela's newspapers every day. His office would have them flown in to Maputo airport on a daily basis. *But over the years they would get lost or left in Nelspruit or on the plane, or never put on the plane in the first place and we were constantly having to explain to the President that there were no papers to read. It never ceased to amaze me at times how shabbily the President was treated by some of his staff. My team members were never allowed to get away with anything less than their very best for Madiba.*

The bodyguards specifically looked forward to these trips as there was very little to do during them but relax and enjoy Maputo, its people and its food. During the process they became extremely friendly with the Mozambican security and shared protection strategies and convoy methods with them. *We loved going there. We always stayed at the beautiful Polana Hotel where there was a gym so that we could train. Madiba was always resting there, so we could take it relatively easy. And the seafood was fantastic.* Also fantastic was the way Graça looked after everyone, including the bodyguards, cooking food for them and really treating them like family. 'Come and join us for supper and forget all your protocol,' was one of her favourite sayings.

Over the last years the bodyguards would constantly comment on what a fitting end to his presidency this relationship was. A woman of grace, elegance, style and deep compassion, Graça is easy to love and admire. And most people would agree that she made a fitting First Lady for South Africa and an ideal companion for the world's favourite president. A reminder to all of us that anything is possible at any age.

“ . . .

A true story as told by
Nelson Mandela

There was a country that wanted to fight a revolutionary war and its leaders went all over the country identifying intelligent young men to serve in this war of liberation. They came to a village in the countryside where they found a man in his forties. He was an opium addict, an alcoholic and he had a sharp eye for pretty young ladies. He spent his life lying around that village, smoking opium and drinking. But once these leaders started talking to this man and discussing their ideas, they realised that here was a very intelligent mind. They sent him to university at the age of forty-something. He was brilliant. Within six months he had completed a three-year course and was made the commander of a small group of soldiers. He did so well that he was quickly promoted and eventually became the overall commander of his country's armed forces, a total of over 250 000 men. That man's name was Chu Teh and the country was the People's Republic of China. (Chu was Chairman Mao's Commander-in-Chief).

. . . ”

EPILOGUE

I said goodbye to President Nelson Mandela outside the lift door of Mahlamba Ndlopfu at 10:40 p.m. on 16 June 1999, his last day as South Africa's first democratically elected president and Thabo Mbeki's first day as its second.

I had effectively served Madiba from Inauguration Day to Inauguration Day, 1994 to 1999. And what years they were! Events experienced, places visited, people met and friends made that have changed my life. I led a wonderful team of men and one woman; a team committed to an incredibly responsible job. We did it well and we had fun.

I worked my last day as an officer in the South African Police Service on 1 August 1999 and retired with the rank of Superintendent. I will always cherish the experience of serving my country as a police officer and the wonderful memories created while doing it. Today I am a director of a company bearing my name and that of my partner, Bob Nicholls. The lessons learnt in providing protection to a living legend, the icon that is Madiba, I can hopefully translate to the corporate environment.

Madiba, my hero, in his own words 'will continue to work for you, my people, for as long as I have breath in my body.' His idea of retirement is continuing a schedule of community projects, charity work and speaking engagements, but at his own pace. I wish him and his beloved wife, Graça, well.

I thank God that I was able to serve Him, my country and this remarkable man in the capacity that I have. It was my desire and is now my fervent prayer that this story be told. It is a story of hope, a story of how one man inspired a nation, dragged it back from the precipice of bloody civil war and taught it to believe in the future. A future not necessarily to be fully realised in my generation, but a bright and glorious one for our children and grandchildren as they grow up without the baggage of our past, in the most beautiful country on earth.

Hamba Kakuhle, Siyabonga Tat'Omkhulu.

GLOSSARY

Abaya – Black robe covering a woman's body from head to ankle height with only a slit for the eyes. Worn by women in Muslim countries.

Advance team – The team of protection officers who secure a venue to be visited by a VIP before the VIP's arrival.

Alpha-page – Press paging system used to advise the media of news conferences etc.

ANC – African National Congress. Founded in 1911 as a voice for black South Africans, banned as an organisation in 1960 and became SA's largest political party, of which Nelson Mandela was president.

Apartheid – Afrikaans, meaning 'seperateness'. This was the official policy and ideology of the National Party since they took power in 1948.

Bakkie – Afrikaans for pick-up or utility vehicle.

Broederbond – Afrikaans, meaning 'brotherhood'. A secret Afrikaner organisation established to further the Afrikaner culture in all levels of SA society. Was particularly powerful in government.

CODESA – Anagram for 'Congress for a Democratic South Africa,' referring to the Kempton Park talks in which the then ruling National Party and the ANC played the lead roles in the transfer of power from the apartheid government.

DIS – Abbreviation of Department of Intelligence and Security of the ANC.

Ekuseni – Zulu for 'in the morning'.

Genadendal – Afrikaans for 'valley of mercy' and the name of the first mission station established in the Cape's so-called coloured community. Also the name of President Mandela's official residence in Cape Town, renamed from the colonial name, Westbrooke.

Hamba – Zulu for 'go' or 'go away'.

Hoe gaan dit? – Traditional Afrikaans greeting, meaning 'how goes it?' (how are you?)

IFP – Inkatha Freedom Party. Started as a Zulu cultural organisation (inkatha is Zulu for 'peace'), became a political party in 1992 under the leadership of Dr. Mangosuthu Buthelezi.

Imbizo – Zulu for meeting or talks.

Inkatha – Zulu for 'peace,' see IFP.

Kaffir – Extremely derogatory name for blacks that has its origins in the British colonial era.

Khulu – See Tata.

Knopkierie – Afrikaans for a wooden stick with a knot of wood or lump at one end, used as a weapon.

Koki pen – Colloquial South African term for felt pen of text pen.

Kraal – Afrikaans for 'corral' for livestock, also a collection of huts surrounded by a fence.

Laager – Afrikaans for a group of ox-wagons drawn into a circle for protection. Commonly used as the term 'laager mentality' meaning a narrow or blinkered and inward-looking viewpoint.

Matric – Abbreviated form of 'matriculation,' which is the school-leaving qualification after 12 years' schooling in SA.

Medic – Term used to refer to the South African Medical Service para-medics assigned to the PPU teams. A doctor would only travel with the team when abroad.

MK – abbreviation for Umkhonto we Sizwe.

Mphokoqo – Xhosa for maize-meal porridge and sour milk.

Number 1 bodyguard – The protector position for the bodyguard who walks immediately behind the VIP and who travels in the VIP's vehicle in the motorcade.

Pointsman – The protector position at the head of the foot formation around a VIP. It is also the convoy leader's position when in the motorcade.

Recce – Abbreviated form of 'reconnaissance,' a military term for checking or scouting an area prior to an operation in that area.

Shosholoza – A Zulu/Ndebele song traditionally sung by workers who labour in unison. It is about a trainload of workers coming from the South. Also traditionally sung at South African cultural or sporting events.

Stratcom – Abbreviated form of 'strategic communication,' meaning an action intended to appear as if it was committed by someone other than the person actually committing it. Usually an action by the State intended to appear to be committed by another entity.

Sun City – A resort-hotel complex of golf courses and casinos built in the bush next to a game reserve in what was the Bantustan of Bophuthatswana (now Northwest Province) as a way around SA's anti gambling laws. The complex now focuses on family entertainment as casinos are legal in SA today.

Swart gevaar – Afrikaans meaning 'black danger,' a term used to refer to a perceived threat to Afrikaner nationalism from black South Africans.

Tata – Short form of the Xhosa word for 'grandfather' which is Tat'Omkhulu. A term of respect, not familiarity.

Tokoloshe – Mythical figure in African custom (similar to a leprechaun). Believed to have spiritual power, is only 6 inches tall, brings bad luck and instills fear. Blacks will traditionally put the feet of their beds on bricks or paint-tins in the belief that the beds will then be too high for the Tokoloshe to get to them.

Umkhonto we Sizwe – Xhosa/Zulu word for 'Spear of the Nation,' the military wing of the African National Congress, co-founded by Nelson Mandela.

Volk en Vaderland – Afrikaans term meaning 'for one's nation/race and fatherland'.